Contents

Foreword ....
The Story of the Book ....
Ways to Use this Book 7
Introduction 9
God 10
Generations 18
Relationships 24
Time 32
Volunteers 38
Gifts 44
Money 50
Possessions 56
Earth 62
Body 70
Mind 76
Vision 82
Conclusion 88
A Narrative of Generosity 92
Endnotes 94
Scripture Index 95

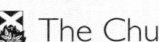

The Church of Scotland

Further information:
Stewardship Team
Stewardship and Finance Department
Church of Scotland

stewardship@churchofscotland.org.uk

www.churchofscotland.org.uk

Foreword
Very Rev Dr W. Martin Fair

Authors
Fiona Penny
Darren Philip
Katherine Southern
Pauline Wilson

Design
Chris Flexen

> **" This new publication... both celebrates what it is to live generously and offers all manner of ways to creatively reflect upon what it looks like and how each of us might embody it.**

Foreword

Very Rev Dr W. Martin Fair

Eric had been a highly successful businessman but lost everything due to a crooked colleague's underhand methods. As a result, he found himself washing dishes in a restaurant kitchen. Scraping by involved Eric and his wife selling every item of value, including her engagement ring, and living without a television and many of the things that most take for granted – all while in his mid-60s. But having heard about the addiction support service that my former congregation ran in Arbroath (though living thousands of miles away), they decided to support us by gifting one-tenth of the little income they had, rather than improving their own situation. Living generously!

One Sunday morning, I announced during worship that a congregation in the east end of Glasgow had been subject to a sustained campaign of vandalism and that on one single night, every single pane of glass in their entire suite of buildings had been broken. I suggested to my own congregation that to offer support and an expression of solidarity, it would be good if we took up an offering for these, our brothers and sisters. Among many others, Janis came to me after the service and gave her whole month's salary. Living generously!

While visiting a small, marginalised Christian community in rural Cambodia – living in abject poverty that surpassed anything I'd seen then or since – our visiting group was invited to sit down for something to eat. We enjoyed a simple dish of chicken and rice and the warmth and welcome of our hosts. Upon leaving, our guide informed us that they had fed us with their only chicken. Imagine our horror in hearing this and yet we were assured that our hosts had done this joyfully, fully believing that God would continue to meet their needs following our departure. Living generously!

Generosity for Christians really is about the way we choose to live – so much more than, but not less than, how much we decide to drop into the offering on Sunday mornings. The attitude of gratitude moves us a million miles away from an approach that is fashioned around 'crumbs from the rich man's table'. It's a lifestyle that begins not from 'what have I got left' but from 'what have I got to start with'.

This new publication, beautifully created by the Church of Scotland's Stewardship Team, both celebrates what it is to live generously and offers all manner of ways to creatively reflect upon what it looks like and how each of us might embody it.

Of course, there are some unhelpful starting points for all of this – not least old-school accusations such as 'the church is aye after your money!' and the idea that money is a private matter. But surely the Christian has to start with a Biblical perspective and, to that end, this book does just that by establishing God's loving generosity as the foundation for all that follows. The nature of God's love calls those who would worship to live generously without ever considering 'what's in it for me?'

And, of course, as many commentators have pointed out, a considerable proportion of what Jesus teaches in the gospels – including nearly half the parables – relates to money and wealth and our attitude to them.

But fear not, this timely book doesn't come at you attempting to guilt-trip you or make you feel bad about yourself! It offers a fresh and liberating way into the question of stewardship, with solid Biblical and theological principles, but without ever getting 'heavy' or burdensome. And critically, it's just as strong on practice as it is on principle, offering a wonderful array of ideas and lived-out experience from a broad range of people and perspectives from across the Church.

Whoever thought a book on stewardship and giving would be such a delight to read! This is exactly that. Read. Enjoy. Be inspired. Live generously.

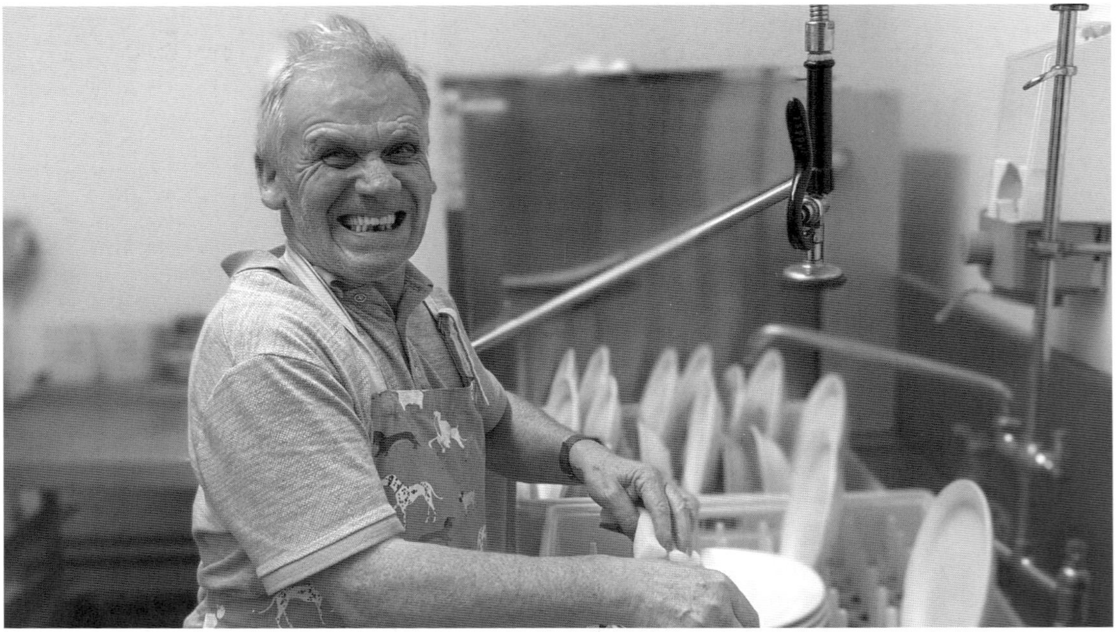

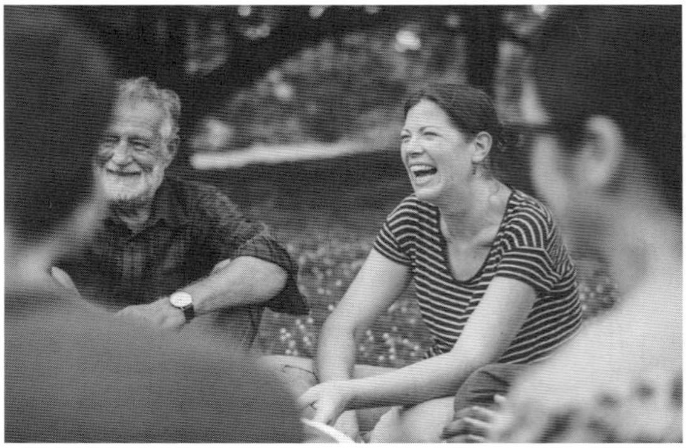

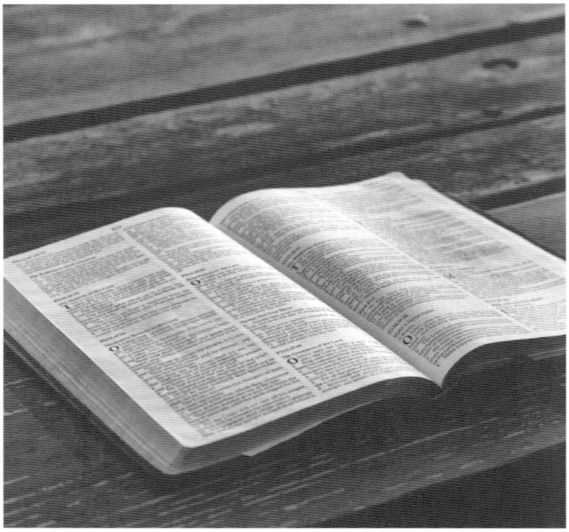

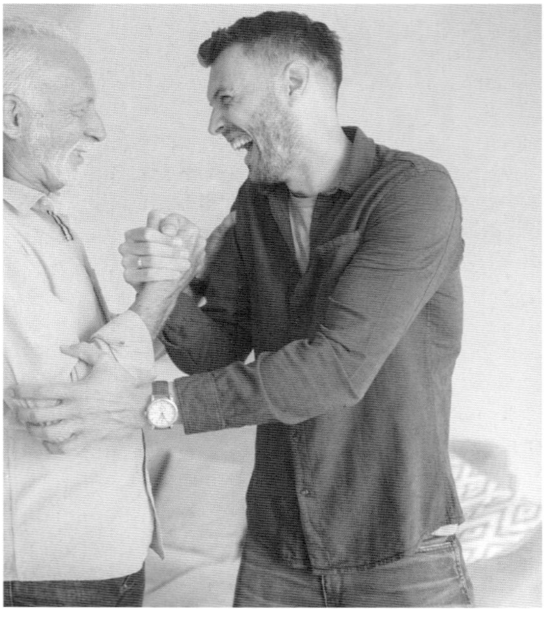

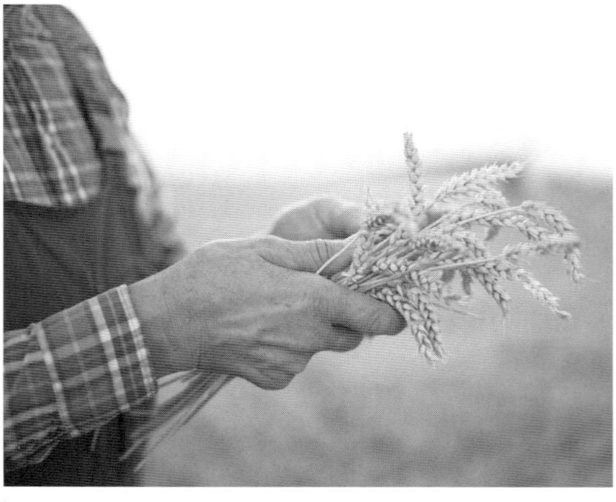

'Living Generously' - The Story of the Book

When we started planning this book, we agreed that it would be a much richer experience – and a more inspirational read – if we involved people from across church communities in the writing process. So, for each theme, we drew on the experiences of folk from different backgrounds and specialisms, usually bringing them together in online conversations with no fixed agenda other than a theme title. Each person brought their own unique perspective, adding breadth and depth to the conversations and encouraging us to branch out into new territory.

These contributors exemplified generosity by giving freely of their time to engage with us – and not just their time, but their thoughtful contributions, their passion and their sense of God's vision for the church and its people. We were so blessed through this process and would like to express our sincere thanks to the following people who contributed in this way:

Rev Jenny Adams, Steve Aisthorpe, Gary Bainbridge, Shirley Billes, Katie Bogie, Rev Andrea Boyes, Rev Lynsey Brennan, Val Brown, Rev David C Cameron, Prof Andrew Clarke, Rev David Coleman, Rev Stewart Cutler, Janet Dick, Mark Evans DCS, Suzi Farrant, Graham Fender-Allison, Rev Dr Richard Frazer, Rev Jim Garrett, Dr Susan Garrett, Robert Gemmell, Lesley Hamilton-Messer, Paul Haringman, Richard Knott, Jo Love DCS, Clare Lucas, Barbara MacFarlane, Ian Matheson, Rev Iain May, Pam Mellstrom, Carolyn Merry, Anne Mulligan DCS, Kirsty Nelson, Rev Dr Sheena Orr, Susan Pym, Ken Reid, Rev Hugh Maurice Stewart, Rev Prof John Swinton, Rev Gayle Taylor, Rev Justin Taylor, Rev William Taylor, Katrona Templeton and Karen Wallace.

As you delve into the book, we hope you will enjoy reading the case studies which are included within the themed chapters. We wanted to demonstrate how the theory is being applied in practice. Across the church, we see people reflecting God's generosity, and we wanted to share the joy of this with you. Be encouraged and inspired by these stories. Perhaps they will highlight some of the ways in which you are already living a generous life; and perhaps they will encourage you to find new ways too. We are so grateful to the following people and projects for allowing us to share their stories:

The 'Spiritual Practices Shared' contributors; Newbattle Church; The Barn Community Café and Livingston Community Shed; Rev David C Cameron; Hot Chocolate Trust; Grassmarket Community Project; Iona Community; Oisean a' Chalman, Uig Church; Eco-Congregation Scotland and Duffus, Spynie and Hopeman Church; Ken Reid; Stonehouse: St Ninian's Church and Hope Café; and Dundonald Church.

The four key writers of the book – Fiona Penny, Darren Philip, Katherine Southern and Pauline Wilson – make up the Church of Scotland's national stewardship team, supporting congregations to be resourced and sustained for mission and ministry.

> "Across the church, we see people reflecting God's generosity, and we wanted to share the joy of this with you.

If you'd like to share your generosity stories with us, please get in touch at:
stewardship@churchofscotland.org.uk

We'd love to hear from you.

Fiona, Darren, Katherine and Pauline

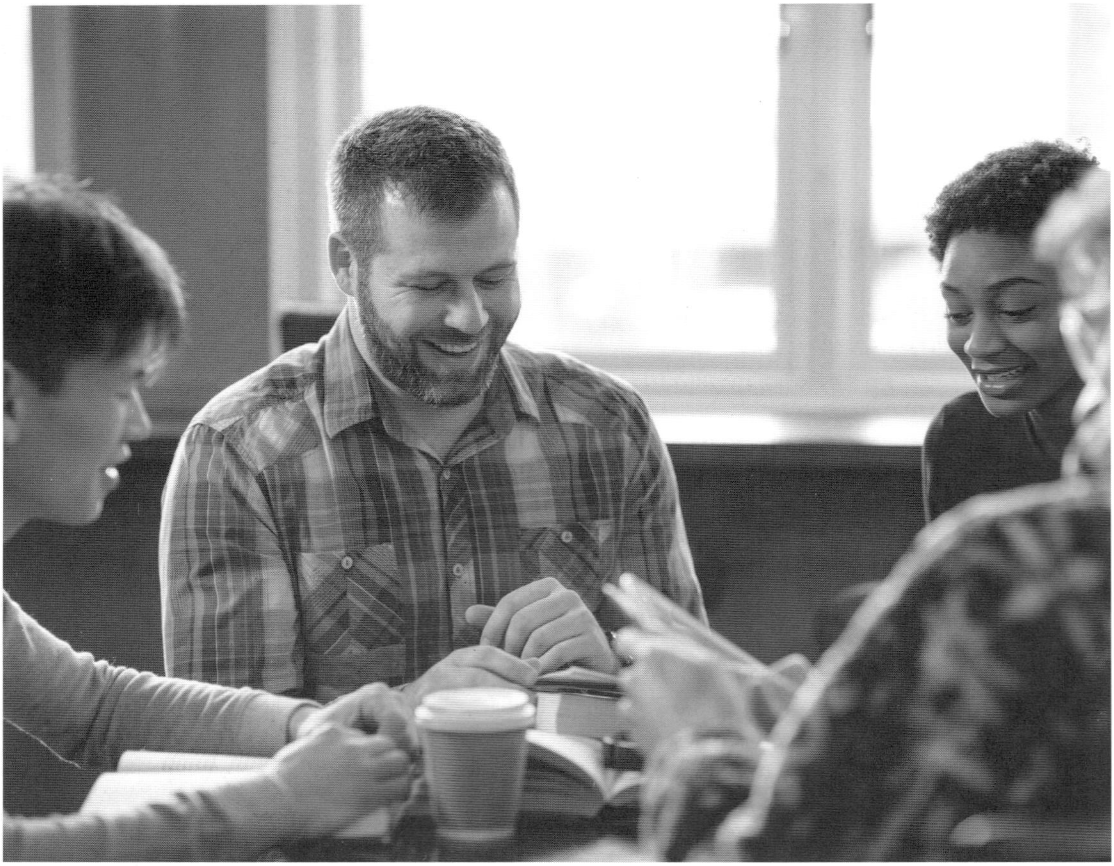

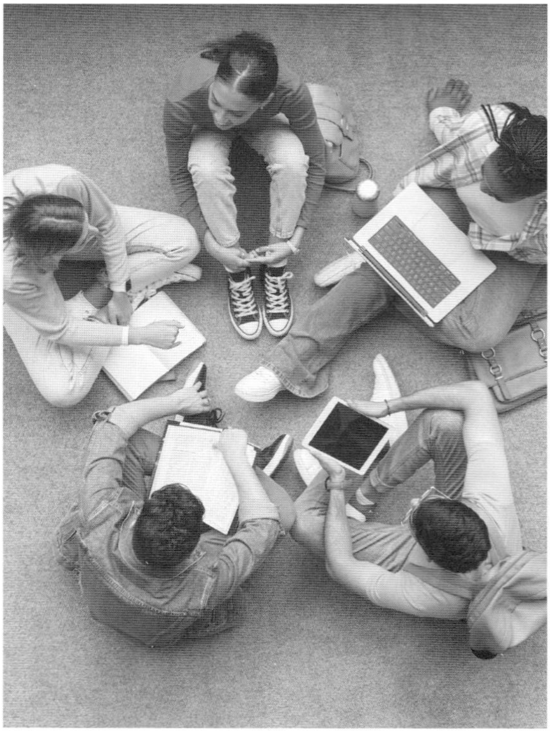

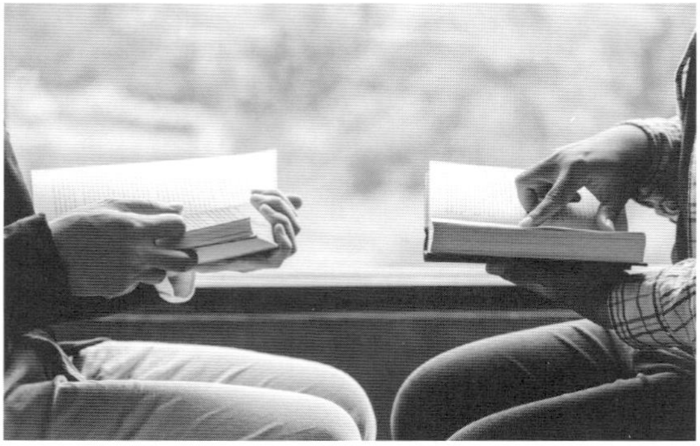

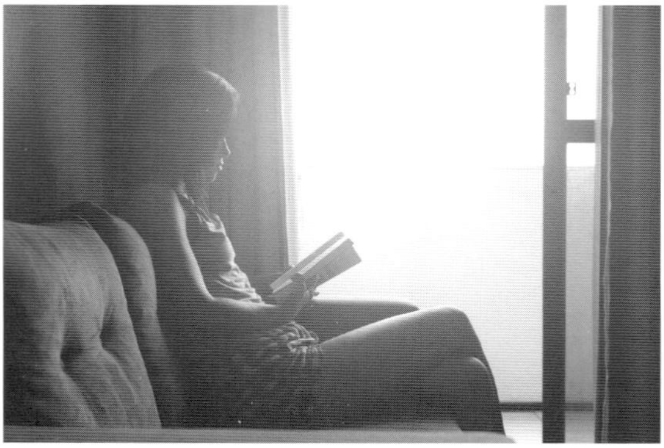

Ways to Use this Book

The aim of this book is to encourage you to consider the practical application of generosity in your life. It is simply a tool for your faith journey, for use by:

- individuals growing in their faith and discipleship practices;
- enquirers and people who are new to faith and church involvement;
- new expressions of church, such as café church, online church, forest church and church plants;
- small groups, such as house groups, Bible study groups or communicants' classes.

Each chapter includes:
- an article which introduces the theme;
- simple prompts to encourage sharing, reflection and action;
- a case study;
- signposts to additional resources including Scripture, books and websites, encouraging you to go deeper into a topic.

You are encouraged to take notes as you go along. If you are using the book in your personal devotions, perhaps you might encourage a friend to do likewise, providing an opportunity for you to share thoughts and reflections with someone else along the way.

In small groups or informal church settings, the prompts encourage people to talk with each other, to share from their own experiences, to hear from others and to learn together.

On page 91 you will find a prayer to support the overall theme of living generously. This can be used within your time of reflection.

The writing team would love to hear how you are using this book, so please do share your stories with them at:
stewardship@churchofscotland.org.uk.

However you choose to use the book, the hope is that it will bear fruit in your life and in the life of the church, and bring glory to God in ways that we can't even imagine. May it help you to 'grasp how wide and long and high and deep is the love of Christ, and to know this love that surpasses knowledge – that you may be filled to the measure of all the fullness of God' (Eph. 3:18b-19).

> "...our natural response to God's giving is generosity.

Introduction

A whole-life response to God's love.

The First Letter to Timothy contains an encouragement not to place our hope in the riches of this world, but in God 'who richly provides us with everything for our enjoyment'. It then speaks of responding to such generosity by being 'rich in good deeds' and being 'generous and willing to share' (1 Tim. 6:17-18). It suggests that our natural response to God's giving is generosity.

This book is aimed at helping you recognise and respond to God's love by living generously in your day-to-day life. The strap-line on the front cover, 'a whole-life response to God's love', summarises what you are about to explore. Let's consider in reverse order the parts that make up that subtitle: God's love, response and whole-life.

God's love

One of the most quoted verses in the Bible comes from John 3:16 – 'For God so loved the world that he gave his one and only Son'. Here we see the link between God's love and generosity: because God loved the world, God gave the most precious thing for it. Scripture is full of stories of God's generosity flowing from love in this way, from the opening chapters of Genesis, where God provides a bountiful world and sees that it is very good (Gen. 1-2) to stories Jesus told about the way God gives food for birds and colour to flowers (Matt. 6:25-30).

Our society often pushes us to desire more, to focus on those things which we do not have or which we want. When we stop for a moment and consider all the ways in which God blesses the world with generosity, we can move beyond perceptions of scarcity and recognise the abundance around us.

Response

How we respond to God's loving generosity matters. This book invites you to consider how, as people made in God's image, we can reflect that generosity in the way we live our lives.

Noticing God's generosity helps us to see that what we 'have' is not really ours: everything belongs ultimately to God. However, God gives it over to us to choose how we make use of it. There's a word which describes caring for and looking after things which don't ultimately belong to us: stewardship. It was a word originally used to refer to caring for the affairs of a household. A steward was someone who decided how best to use those things which were entrusted to them. Stewardship is an important concept in being a follower of Jesus. It means acknowledging that everything we have comes ultimately from God and discerning how best to use it for God's purposes in the world.

Whole-life

Stewardship applies to the whole of our lives. There is a deliberately broad mix of themes in this book, aimed at helping you recognise and respond to God's generosity in different aspects of life. The themes presented here are all signs of God's generosity – and are real-life subjects which we encounter every day. They are: God, generations, relationships, time, volunteers, gifts, money, possessions, earth, body, mind and vision.

There are many more themes which could have been chosen, and hopefully the model of 'think/share-reflect-act' is one which will help you explore other subjects too. Following Jesus affects the way life is lived, so much so that in the book of Acts the earliest followers of Jesus were known as 'The Way'. The chapters that follow are designed to help you reflect on how you can live as part of 'The Way' in a whole-life response to God's love.

GOD

Developing and nurturing a two-way relationship with God

> **"** Isn't it amazing that we each see and experience God differently and that there is always more of God to be found?

A Closer Walk

One of the privileges of discipleship is that, through Christ, we have direct access to God. What an amazing gift! How can we cherish and foster our relationship with God in a way which reflects God's generosity towards us?

Elizabeth Barrett Browning's sonnet 43 begins:
   How do I love thee? Let me count the ways.
   I love thee to the depth and breadth and height my soul can reach...

This poem was written about human love, but imagine for a moment that God is speaking those words direct to you. Do they resonate with you? Are you able to accept that God loves you in this way? In Paul's letter to the Ephesians, he prays that the Lord's people may grasp how wide and long and high and deep is the love of Christ, a love that, he goes on to say, surpasses knowledge (Eph. 3:17-19). Paul's suggestion is that, while God's love is a mystery far beyond what we can completely understand, we can capture something of it and so 'be filled with all the fullness of God'. This is a continuous process of growth, participation and discovery. The Message paraphrase expresses it like this: 'Reach out and experience the breadth! Test its length! Plumb the depths! Rise to the heights! Live full lives, full in the fullness of God.'

It's true that God's love for us is not dependent on what we think, do or say, but having a living, breathing, transformational relationship with God does require our participation. We are invited into relationship.

The logic we apply to our relationships with the people we love applies to our relationship with God too. Developing, nurturing and sustaining a close and fulfilling connection with someone requires that commitment is mutual, communication is key, and love is the motivation.

Returning to the sonnet, imagine yourself saying those same words back to God. Do these expressions ring true? Is love for God at the heart of your faith? Does it motivate you to seek God and look for new revelations of God's character? Does it inspire you to stretch your devotional muscle beyond the habitual practices you may have adopted? Whether you are new to faith or further along in your discipleship adventures, this 'How do I love thee' question is worthy of reflection if we are to deepen our relationship with God and be filled with God's goodness.

Every relationship with God is unique, and so the practices we adopt to nurture this will also differ. There are, however, well-worn, proven paths which many have walked over the centuries. Some are paths of active engagement such as prayer, Bible reading and study, while others are paths of abstinence such as silence, solitude and fasting. Developing a rhythm or routine can form the basis of our regular connection with God, but there is something to be said for branching off into less familiar territories too – for exploring and experimenting, whether within our comfort-zone or pushing its boundaries. In our devotional lives, there can be both blessing in consistency and wisdom in change.

Just as each relationship with God is unique, how we each think of and describe God will vary too, influenced by our nature, background and experiences. Isn't it amazing that we each see and experience God differently and that there is always more of God to be found? Breanna Alverson describes God in this way: 'God is my diamond. He is my rock, my forever, my gift and my treasure. As I ponder and consider His character, carefully examining each face of His intricate self, I am in awe of all that He is.'[1]

Imagining God in this way, like a diamond, can be very helpful: every person, looking from their own perspective, sees a different facet. And as we progress through life, we glimpse different aspects or dimensions: the way you think about God today is probably different from how you thought about God ten years ago, twelve months ago or even yesterday. As we listen and learn and grow, so our understanding and experience of God grow too. There is so much of God to know, so many aspects of God's character with which to engage, and so much that is beyond even our most creative imaginings.

God has blessed us with a love which extends beyond anything we can ever imagine. Responding in generosity as stewards of our faith involves entering into a life-long relationship with God and finding devotional practices which aid us on a journey of discovery. Whichever aspects of God we glimpse will, for now, only be partial. As we are told in 1 Corinthians 13:12, 'For now we see only a reflection as in a mirror; then we shall see face to face. Now I know in part; then I shall know fully, even as I am fully known.'

THINK/SHARE:

Take time to:

- look at the photographs on pages 14 and 15 and select one which conveys something to you about God or your relationship with God
- think/share about the ways in which you currently connect with God and how helpful these have been in developing a healthy and fulfilling two-way relationship
- share with someone or make a note of the significant moments in your relationship with God.

REFLECT:

Reflect on your own experiences or the stories you have heard from others on this theme. Now read Psalm 103.

Consider:

- which lines from this Psalm speak to you today and why
- the analogy of God as a diamond with many angles and facets
- what led you to select the picture you chose earlier, and what pictures you might have selected at different times in your life
- how your perception of God has developed and what has influenced your understanding.

'Praise the Lord, my soul; all my inmost being, praise his holy name.'
(Ps. 103:1)

ACT:

Having reflected on God's generosity in inviting us into relationship, how will you respond?

Consider:
- taking on or letting go of something that will help your relationship with God grow
- sharing with someone your story of how you engage with God
- organising or attending an event involving speakers who may inspire people to connect with God in different ways.

RESOURCES:

Scripture:
Deuteronomy 4:1-31
Psalm 1
Philippians 4:4-9
Hebrews 10:19-25

Books:

Church of Scotland, **Conversations in Prayer** (Edinburgh: Mission and Discipleship Council, 2018)

Henri Nouwen, **Discernment: Reading the Signs of Daily Life** (London: SPCK, 2013)

Jack Levison, **40 Days with the Holy Spirit: Fresh Air for Every Day** (Brewster: Paraclete Press, 2015)

Diana Butler Bass, **Freeing Jesus: Rediscovering Jesus as Friend, Teacher, Savior, Lord, Way and Presence** (New York: HarperOne, 2021)

Paul S. Minear, **Images of the Church in the New Testament** (Louisville: Westminster John Knox Press, 2004)

Susan R. Garrett and Amy Plantinga Pauw, **Making Time for God: Daily Devotions for Children and Families to Share** (Grand Rapids: Baker Books, 2002)

Websites:
Practicing Our Faith – **practicingourfaith.org**
24-7 Prayer – **24-7prayer.com**
Prayer Eleven – **prayereleven.org**

Apps:

Bible in One Year
Guardians of Ancora (a Bible based game for 8-11 year olds, Scripture Union)
Lectio 365

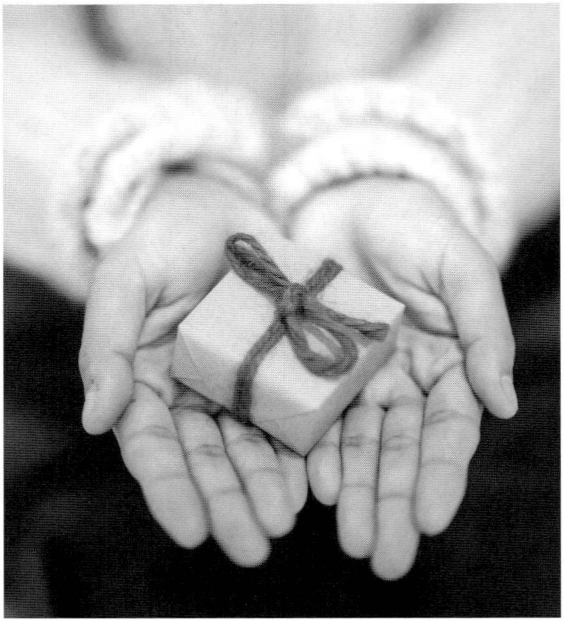

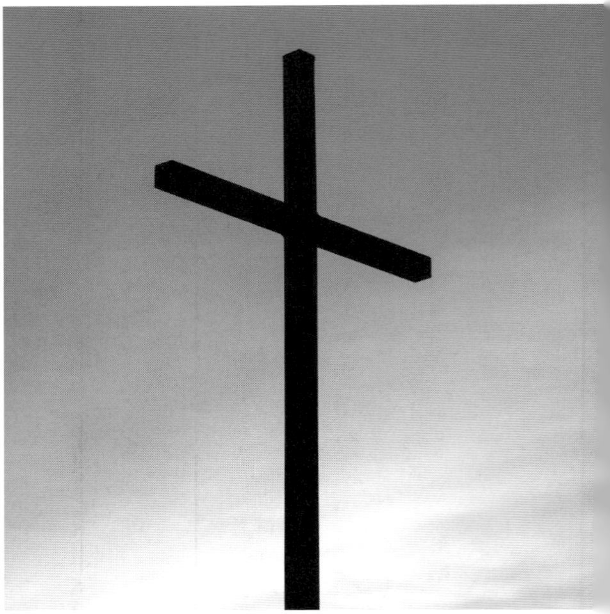

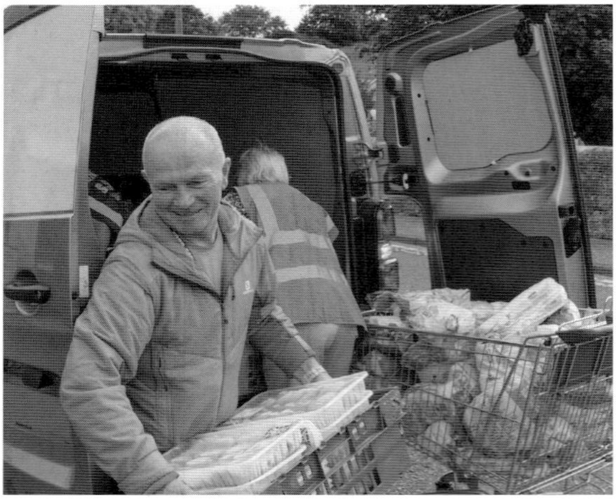

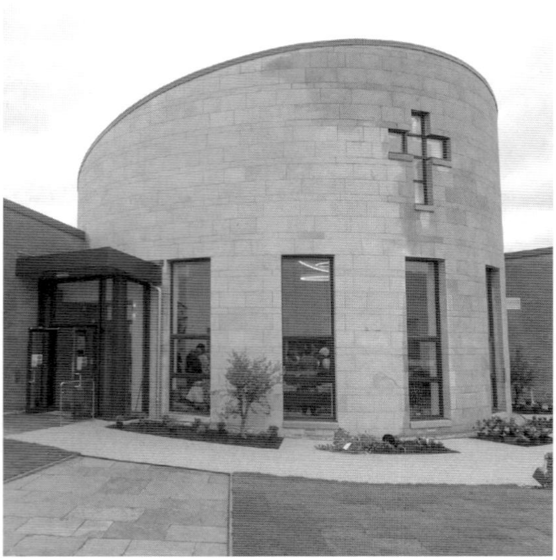

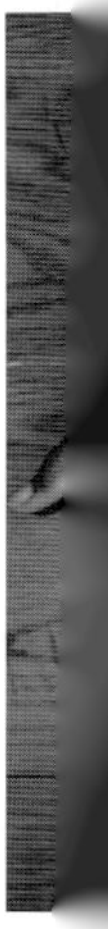

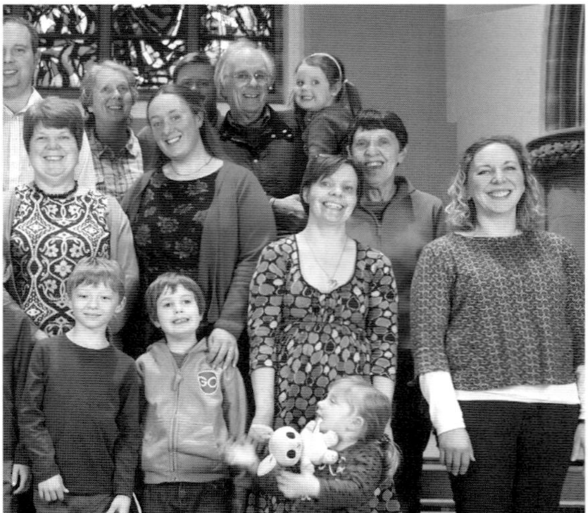

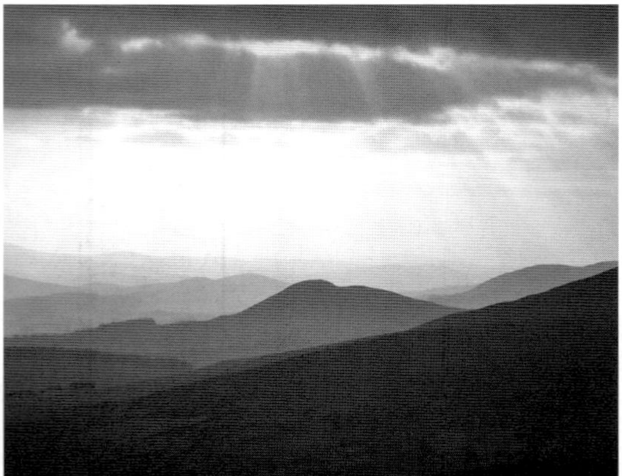

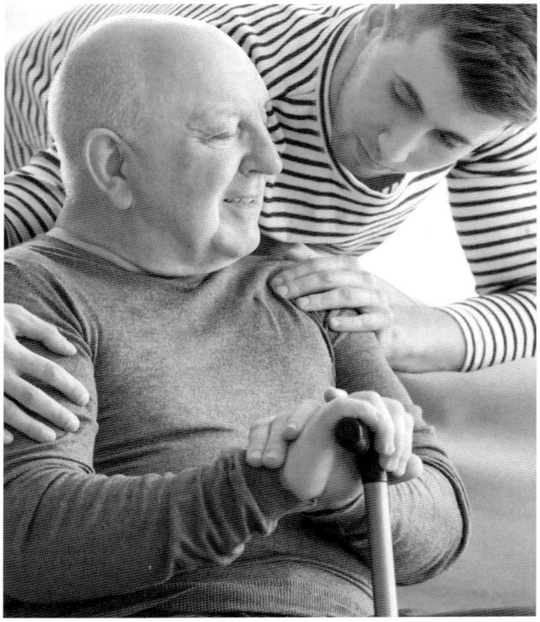
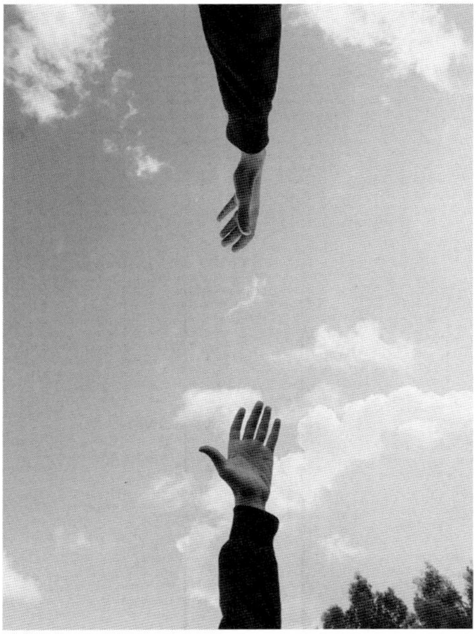
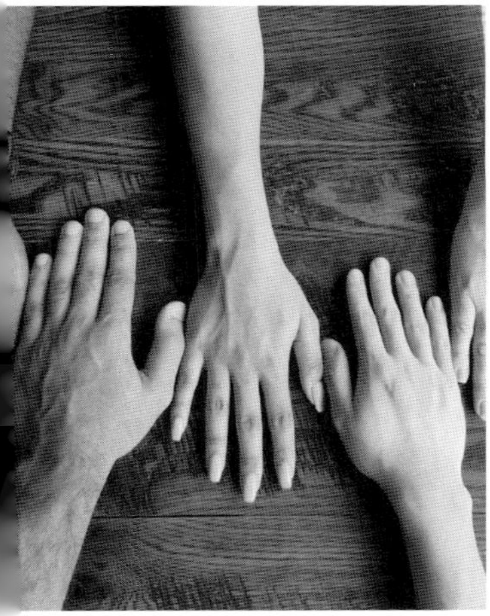
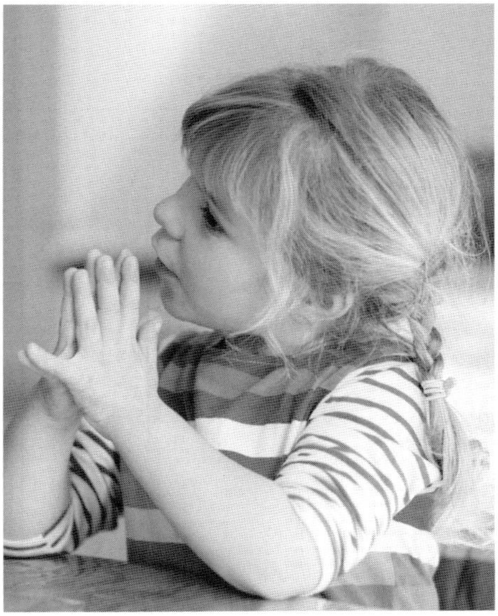
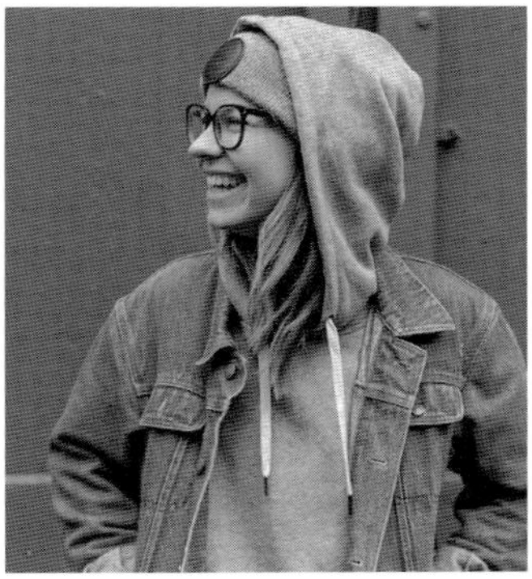
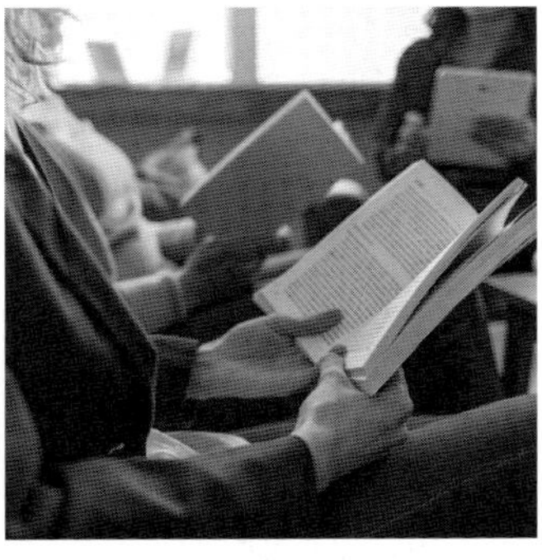
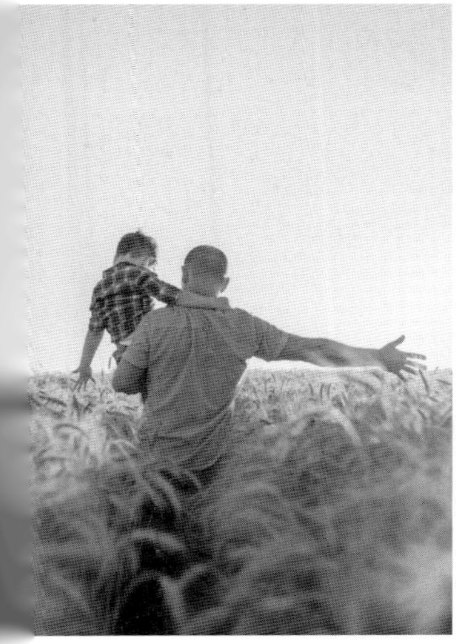
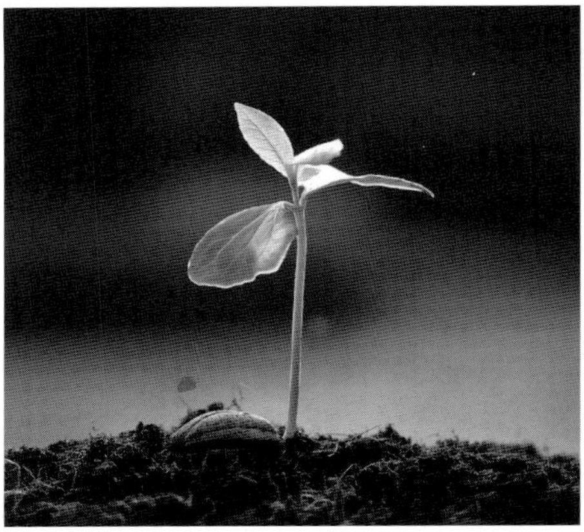
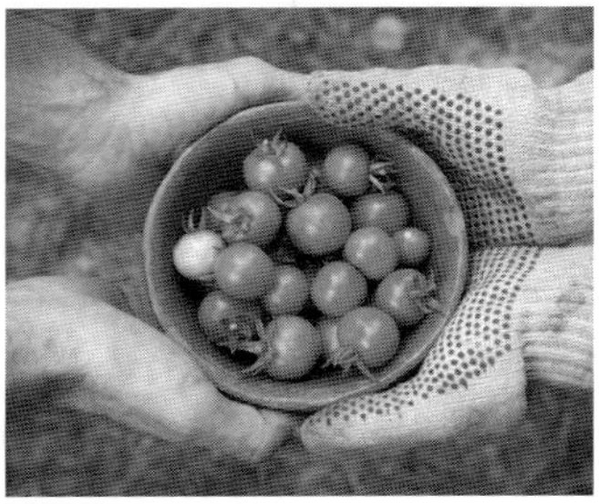

Case Study

> " Hearing about other people's journeys of faith... enhances mine.

Let Me Count the Ways

Spiritual Practices Shared

We can nurture and deepen our relationship with God in so many different and varied ways. Here's a selection of approaches others have found helpful:

- I personally find that routine is at the heart of my connection with God, although I have at times been involved in more experimental prayer groups. My personal daily prayer takes two forms:

    (1) Journeying Prayer: Wherever I am going, I pray for everything I pass on the way e.g. local school, hospital, shops, and all the people there and any issues which they may be experiencing.

    (2) S.T.O.P. Prayer: Sorry (confession); Thanks (thanksgiving); Offering (what I can give in service); Please (intercession). I often use this at the end of the day. It works well with young folks/children. (Marian)

- I have found starting each day with a time of silence and conscious breathing very beneficial. Connecting with the breath, the life-force, relaxes my body and takes me out of my head which is full of thoughts. Dropping into a meditative state, I remember that I am not my thoughts, or the feelings associated with them. Observing my thoughts and allowing them to pass through brings about a feeling of expansion and a sense that everything in life is held by a loving God. I conclude these periods of conscious breathing with a time of gratitude for the gift of life. (Rolf)

- Each morning, when I walk my dogs around some fields, I take the opportunity to practice adoration and gratitude towards God. I also pray for family, friends and situations I have read about in the news. I preview the day ahead and ask the Lord to give me his help and strength. In the evening, before I go to bed, I practice the Examen. I review my day, giving thanks for blessings received and offering confession for mistakes I have made. I also use John Baillie's *Diary of Private Prayer*. (Ken)

- I tend to find a practice which keeps me going for a wee while, but I then sense the need for something different to sustain me for the next while. As someone once so helpfully put it: 'what keeps us alive is not the best practice but the next practice'. Currently, every morning at breakfast, I light a tea-light candle, change the date on my cube calendar (a gift with its own significance as it came from my best friend) and greet the new day, with hello God, or maybe the Lord's Prayer, or quietness. Sometime near the end of each day, I write one line on my wall calendar, noting some event or emotion of that day, whether joyful, special, ordinary or tough, and say thanks for God's presence in it. Unusually for me, this might actually keep me going for a whole year! (Jo)

- What has helped me is listening to different podcasts. I was able to complete the Bible for the first time last year with Daily Audio Bible. This year I'm using Ten Minute Bible Hour which looks at each passage in much more detail which I'm really enjoying. Having friends and a husband who are Christians and being able to talk about sermons and different aspects of the Bible together in social gatherings and small groups really helps me too, as does taking part in a choir and just being involved in church. (Jenni)

- Hearing about other people's journeys of faith, regardless of their faith, enhances mine. Immersing myself in my garden, surrounded by the ever changing colours, sounds and smells of God's glorious creation, feeds my soul. And listening to or singing songs of faith always leaves me spiritually refreshed and re-energised, especially songs that challenge or question, or have sublime melodies and give me goosebumps. (Sue)

- An essential for me is attending a monthly 'Filling Station' and its annual festival 'Refuel'. The Filling Station provides an informal opportunity to meet with others in the presence of the Holy Spirit. It's a time where I worship, listen, reflect, receive prayer and hear what God is speaking into my life enabling me to be 'filled up', refreshed and equipped to step back out into the world again. (Fiona)

- Music draws me closer to God, connecting with my head, heart and soul. The songs I use are often taken straight from Scripture. Not only do they help me to focus on God, but the words set to melody stay with me and come to mind when I'm in need of them. (Anne)

GENERATIONS

Recognising all ages and stages of life as a blessing to the Church

> " Bringing generations together combines age-old insight and fresh perspective...

The Whole People of God

Every age and stage of life is a gift from God. People from all generations play a valuable role in the life of the church.

In Luke 2:41-50, there's a story that is every parent's worst nightmare: on a journey home from a big city, Jesus' mum and dad become aware he is missing. It takes three days and a complete retracing of their steps before they discover him sitting in the temple, speaking with the teachers there.

Jesus is 12 years old – a year before his bar mitzvah coming-of-age, so he would be very much still regarded as a child by his community. Despite his young age, the great teachers of the temple make time to speak with him and wrestle with his questions. They are also 'amazed' at the understanding he shows. Neither the age of the adults nor the youthfulness of Jesus presents a barrier to engaging with one another.

Looking back to the beginning of the story, it becomes clear that this coming together of generations was not just a one-off occurrence in the temple. How did Jesus' parents not notice that he had stayed behind? Their community of faith did not travel as individual household units, but together as one people. Children, therefore, would often spend time with friends or relatives in the group rather than with their parents. There was an assumption that caring for each other, even the youngest, was everyone's responsibility.

Instructions from Scripture like 'These commands that I give to you today are to be on your hearts. Impress them on your children' (Deut. 6:6-7a) and 'Teach them to your children and to their children after them' (Deut. 4:9b) were addressed to the whole faith community, not just parents. The philosophy of the faith community was like the African proverb: 'It takes a village to raise a child'. Everyone, regardless of age, belonged to the community and, as such, was the responsibility of the whole community.

There is much wisdom in this approach. Belonging is an essential foundation to faith formation and is for many people the entry point to a life of discipleship. Feeling a sense of belonging to a faith community provides the security and space in which to explore the beliefs and practices of that community.

Even a very young child can feel a sense of belonging to their church family, and so is already on this path of discipleship – children are disciples, not disciples in the making. The same is true at the opposite end of life when memory and body can begin to falter – belonging is the anchor which holds someone firmly in the community of faith.

Responding generously to people of other generations requires recognising every stage of life as a blessing. We all have our own part to play in ensuring that everyone feels they belong in the church family regardless of age. God promises to work through people of all ages. Joel 2:28 says, for example, 'I will pour out my spirit on all people. Your sons and daughters will prophesy, your old folk will dream dreams, your young folk will see visions'. As stewards of the whole people of God, our task is to build up the faith of the whole body of Christ: supporting and nurturing people who are young, old and everywhere in between.

Research has shown that teenagers are more likely to make a life-long commitment to faith when there are five or more adults within the church who are invested in their lives.[2] The same is true across the age spectrum. Fostering a sense of belonging for all ages involves investing ourselves in one another's lives. At its most basic level, this involves taking the time to learn the names, interests, passions and concerns of others across the age spectrum of your congregation. Taking it further, it means participating in life together with others, sharing the highs, the lows and everything in between. It also means enabling all ages to go beyond the church family and into the wider community, playing their part as both disciples and disciple-makers.

A spirit of generosity towards those of other ages requires us to see things from their perspective. This may challenge our preconceived ideas of what church looks like. Do we believe and expect that God can use and speak to us through those who are much younger or older? How could the church enable everyone to contribute the gifts of their generation in a way that enhances worship, learning and decision-making? Bringing generations together combines age-old insight and fresh perspective, and recognises that God's generosity extends across the whole of life.

THINK/SHARE:

Tell someone or make a note of a time when:

- an interaction with someone of a different generation has been particularly powerful
- you have been inspired or helped in your faith by someone much younger or older than you
- you were encouraged to do something or entrusted with responsibility as a young person.

REFLECT:

Reflect on your own experiences or the stories you have heard from others on this theme. Now read 1 Corinthians 12:12-27.

Consider:

- how this passage speaks to your understanding of the place of different generations in the church
- what church life might look like if people of different ages had 'equal concern for each other' (v. 25)
- how you could help foster a sense of belonging across generations.

'Those parts of the body that seem to be weaker are indispensable'.
(1 Cor. 12:22)

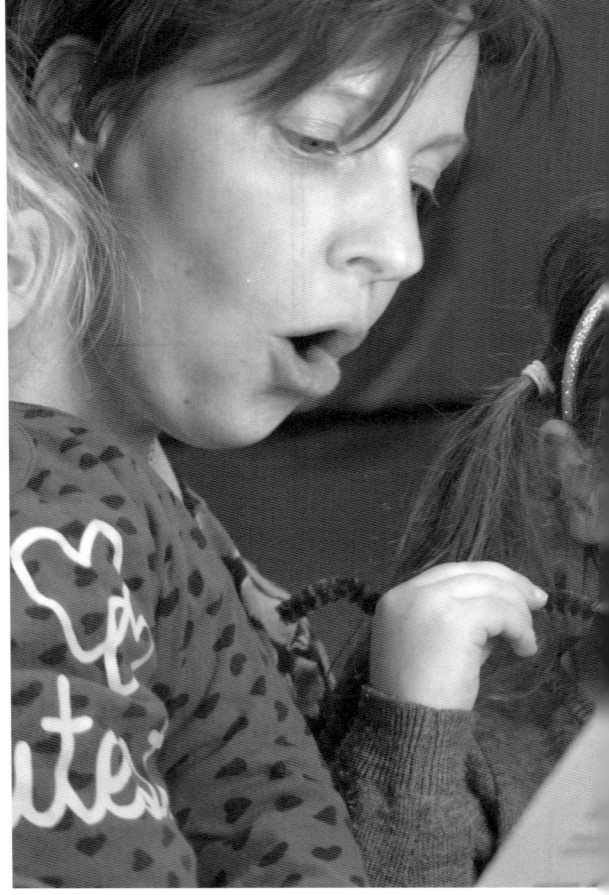

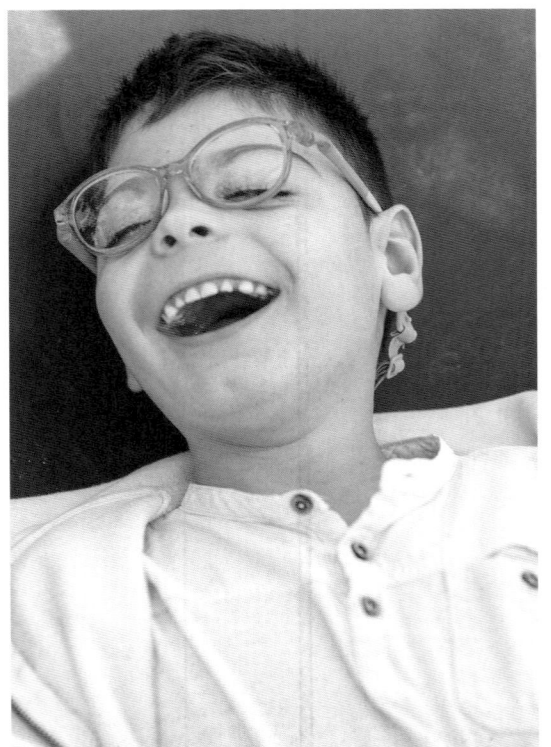

ACT:

Having reflected on God's generosity across generations, how will you respond?

Consider:
- beginning a conversation with someone of a different generation to whom you wouldn't usually speak
- hosting an intergenerational event or gathering, involving people of all ages in its planning and delivery
- connecting with community groups which benefit different generations, such as youth clubs or seniors' groups
- keeping in mind other generations as you reflect on the range of themes in this book.

RESOURCES:

Scripture:
Psalm 145

Books:
Catherine Falconer, **How Will Our Children Have Faith?** (Edinburgh: Saint Andrew Press, 2015)

Suzi Farrant and Darren Philip, **Being an Intergenerational Church: Practices to Bring the Generations Back Together**, (Edinburgh: Saint Andrew Press, 2023)

Holly Catterton Allen, Christine Lawton and Cory L. Seibel, **Intergenerational Christian Formation: Bringing the Whole Church Together in Ministry, Community, and Worship**, (Downers Grove: IVP, 2023)

David M. Csinos, **A Gospel for All Ages: Teaching and Preaching with the Whole Church**, (Minneapolis: Fortress Press, 2022)

Websites:
Generations Working Together – **generationsworkingtogether.org**

Messy Church – **messychurch.org.uk**

Other:
Exploring Generosity – resources from the Church of Scotland Stewardship Team to explore the themes of this book intergenerationally.

Case Study

> "...taking the time to know everyone by name, taking an interest in what life is like for them and entrusting everyone with some responsibility and ownership.

Safe, Supported and Spiritual

Newbattle Parish Church

Transition ministry supports a congregation through a period of change. Rev Gayle Taylor describes this as primarily involving a shift in mindset: 'When a congregation opts for transition ministry, they agree to focus on what they can do rather than what they can't, and to cultivate a "Yes, we can do that" attitude'.

Newbattle Parish Church, where Gayle serves, has embraced this outlook resulting in a transformation in their buildings, pattern of worship and connection with the local community. This change of mindset is perhaps most clearly seen in the approach the congregation has taken to fostering relationships across generations.

Like many congregations, the majority of Newbattle's worshipping congregation were beyond retirement age. Gayle's previous role specialised in ministry with children and young people, so it might have been hard for her to come to a congregation where few children were present, but she doesn't see it that way. 'Churches often say they have no children,' she says, 'but everyone in the church has children in their lives and there are children in the community'.

By working as a chaplain in local schools, Gayle has opened a way for the church to provide pastoral and practical support to pupils and their families. Through assemblies and services; targeted work with pupils who have additional needs; provision of school holiday food parcels in partnership with the Trussell Trust; a Food Initiative providing hot meals for different age groups and Ukrainian families; a Wednesday Community Café; and 'New2U' shop, the congregation can live out its vision of offering 'a safe, supportive and spiritual place at the heart of the community'.

As well as offering targeted groups for children (such as the 'JAM Club' which meets in the church after school), the congregation has worked to foster a sense of belonging across the whole of church life. When the church was vandalised by a small group of young people, Gayle was able to use her links with the school to understand the socio-economic circumstances these young people were facing. Rather than turn to the criminal justice system, the congregation was able to work in partnership with the neighbouring youth project to relate to young people hanging about around the shops and church. By creating opportunities for activity and conversation in the school holidays, the congregation invited them into relationship, offering care and raising awareness. For example, one young person was impressed that the church was a 'warm bank' throughout the winter. This changed the idea of the church just being a building to the reality of it being 'a place that our community needs' – where good things happen and people are helped.

These links have also opened the way for young people from the local high school to volunteer at the church's afternoon Men's Group. Whether through serving and sharing lunch, or simple activities such as playing draughts together, this has cultivated deep relationships of belonging across generations. Each brings the unique gifts of their generation as a blessing to the other: older generations have time to offer and skills to share, while younger generations bring a natural inquisitiveness and energy which has caused everyone to learn and grow. In these relationships, the fruit of the Spirit are demonstrated: love, joy, peace, patience, kindness, goodness, faithfulness, gentleness and self-control (Gal. 5:22-23).

'I feel really welcome here' says one teenager, while another responds that 'It just means so much that you're interested in me'. How does the congregation work to develop this sense of belonging for all ages? Gayle identifies three important features among others: taking the time to know everyone by name, taking an interest in what life is like for them and entrusting everyone with some responsibility and ownership. One young man's remark that 'It meant a lot when you trusted me with your keys – that was a big thing for me', demonstrates how even the smallest acts can help develop a sense of belonging.

The adults involved in Newbattle's Men's Group, Food Initiative, New2U Shop and Café may not think of themselves as youth workers, but their 'Yes, we can do that' mindset has enabled them to create a safe, supportive and spiritual place of belonging for all generations.

RELATIONSHIPS

Nurturing and prioritising our relationships

> **"** If relationship is at the heart of who God is then humans, being made in God's image, are made for relationship.

Being Perceptive, Present and Proactive

How do you usually respond when someone asks, 'How are you?' Most of us answer, 'Fine, thanks' or, 'Not bad, thank you', as we assume the question is simply a passing pleasantry. It is often only in our closest relationships that we open up honestly to each other. But what if we offered that deeper level of interest and attentiveness to everyone, reflecting more of God in every encounter?

God's very nature is relationship. We know one God as three persons – Father, Son and Holy Spirit – in the relationship known as the Trinity. If relationship is at the heart of who God is then humans, being made in God's image, are made for relationship. In Galatians 5:22-23, Paul lists nine qualities of a person who lives in unity with the Holy Spirit. These 'fruit' are all relational terms: love, joy, peace, patience, kindness, goodness, faithfulness, gentleness and self-control. In other words, living in accord with God's Spirit is demonstrated through our relationships with other people. The way we relate to one another is a hallmark of our discipleship.

Stories in Scripture of God walking alongside others offer us a model for relationship. In Genesis 3:8, Adam and Eve encountered God walking in the garden; in the Exodus, God led the Hebrew people to wander in the wilderness for forty years; after the events of the first Easter, the risen Jesus drew alongside those walking the road to Emmaus (Luke 24:13-35). This pattern of God meeting people as they walked on their journey offers a model of relationship that is about presence rather than power, interest rather than influence. In relating to people by being fully present to them, we reflect the nature of God. As it is put in The Message paraphrase, God 'comes alongside us when we go through hard times, and… brings us alongside someone else who is going through hard times so that we can be there for that person just as God was there for us' (2 Cor. 1:4).

How, then, might we respond to this gift of relationship? How might we steward our relationships well, displaying the fruit of the Spirit in our interactions? There are many ways to relate well, but three practices are offered here which can help develop a depth of relationship: be perceptive, be present and be proactive.

Being perceptive means noticing all the opportunities we have for relationship as we go about our lives. When thinking of 'relationships', it is easy to think only of our family and friends, or those we get to know well such as work colleagues or our church family. The relationships Jesus struck up in the gospels were often, however, with people he didn't know. He dined with, healed and invited strangers because he 'saw' them (see, for example, Luke 19:1-9, Mark 10:46-52 and Matthew 4:18-22). He was perceptive enough to notice the opportunity for relationship. In our everyday lives, we can also choose to relate well to those we encounter: the cashier in the supermarket, the bus driver, the neighbour down the road. Relationships don't have to be long-standing to reflect God's nature: God is present in every interaction we have with another.

Being present involves creating space for each relationship to develop. It means meeting people where they are and coming alongside them, eager to learn from the other rather than assuming we understand. Being present means being non-judgemental, desiring the best for someone without trying to change who they are, 'hanging in there' with them if things get tough. Being present recognises others as bearing God's image and responds to them accordingly, for whatever we do to others it is as if we were doing it to Christ (Matt. 25:31-46).

Being proactive recognises that relationships – all relationships – require attentiveness. Often, we only think about working on our relationships when they begin to go wrong. Taking a more proactive approach helps us to sustain and build our relationships well. There can be a temptation to ignore differences or difficult situations, but addressing these together in love builds respect and can leave our relationships stronger. Acknowledging difference not only avoids conflict, but draws us closer as we come to understand more of the other and their circumstances. Whether we agree with the other person or not, proactively exploring our relationship allows us to hear and understand the other's story, while opening our story to them.

Our different stories and relationships are held within and shaped by the larger, more loving story of God's love. When we show love in our relationships, we participate in that eternal story.

THINK/SHARE:

Tell someone or make a note of a time when:

- you struck up a meaningful conversation with someone unexpected
- you were supported by someone who came alongside you
- you took positive action to nurture or heal a relationship.

REFLECT:

Reflect on your own experiences or the stories you have heard from others on this theme. Now read Philippians 2:1-11.

Consider:
- the relational qualities mentioned in the passage
- how your relationship with God shapes your relationships with others
- how you might honour God through your relationships.

'In your relationships with one another, have the same mindset as Christ Jesus.' (Phil. 2:5)

ACT:

Having reflected on God's generosity in the area of relationships, how will you respond?

Consider:

- asking God to make you more perceptive and sensitive in your daily interactions with others
- making a special effort to prioritise a relationship that has been neglected
- working with others to organise a social gathering for your church and community, providing an opportunity for relationships to form and grow
- making time to get alongside people you may not naturally associate with, to better understand their circumstances and perspectives

RESOURCES:

Scripture:

John 13:34-35
1 Corinthians 13:1-7
Ephesians 4:25-32

Books:

Jared Byas, **Love Matters More: How Fighting to be Right Keeps Us from Loving Like Jesus** (Grand Rapids, Michigan: Zondervan, 2020)

Henri Nouwen, **The Return of the Prodigal Son: A Story of Homecoming** (London: Darton, Longman and Todd, 1992)

Kara K Root, **The Deepest Belonging: A Story About Discovering Where God Meets Us** (Minneapolis: Fortress Press, 2021)

Desmond and Mpho Tutu, **The Book of Forgiving: The Fourfold Path for Healing Ourselves and the World** (London: William Collins, 2014)

Websites:

Care for the Family – **careforthefamily.org.uk**

Place for Hope – **placeforhope.org.uk**

Case Study

A Place Where Everyone Knows Your Name

The Barn Community Café and Livingston Community Shed

In 2021, when socialising was still constrained by the Covid-19 pandemic and many venues were closing down, Livingston United Parish Church opened The Barn Community Café. Recognising the high levels of isolation within the community, project manager Norma Brown was keen to provide a space for people to meet safely and build relationships.

Visitors are viewed as more than customers, with volunteers deliberately working to build connections between people. Anne, who started coming with her late husband following his diagnosis with dementia, can attest to this:

'I found the café to be a place where we could both feel safe and relaxed, when other places might not be so welcoming. Very quickly, the staff and volunteers got to know us and would be understanding of my husband's illness. Now that I am on my own, I still come every week. If I go to a café in town, I sit alone, looking at my phone or reading my book like everyone else. When I come here, people know my name. When my usual friends aren't around, I can join any table and know that I'll be welcomed.'

Bob, another regular, came into contact with The Barn shortly after it opened:

'I was cutting through the church grounds on my way to the supermarket, just a few weeks after my wife had passed away. I noticed that there was a buzz around the place, but just continued on for my shopping. On the way back, I stopped again to take another look. This time, I was spotted by Norma who encouraged me to come in and to sit with a group of three men who were already chatting together. It turned out they had all been widowed over recent months, just like me, so we immediately had something in common. After that first visit, I went back every Monday and Friday and would sit with the same group. We got to know each other and, I guess, supported each other in our own way.'

After a few weeks of seeing the men meet up in this way, Norma approached them with an idea: 'I thought they might welcome having something more structured to do. I had heard about the Men's Sheds Association and wondered if it would work in our community. I set up a visit to another Shed project and we were all impressed by it, though we agreed to include women in our project so that everyone who wanted to join could do so.'

Livingston Community Shed now meets weekly to do gardening and DIY projects in different communities around the town, recently winning a 'Helping Your Community Grow' award run by a nearby garden centre. The work itself is fulfilling and is making a difference in local neighbourhoods, but the project's main purpose is to encourage and nurture good relationships.

'We have a lot of banter with one another,' explains Bob. 'While working away, we're always talking, always getting to know one another. I feel like I've had some of these friends my whole life.'

> "While working away, we're always talking, always getting to know one another. I feel like I've had some of these friends my whole life."

For more information about The Barn, visit **lupc.org.uk**, and for information about the Men's Sheds Association, visit **menssheds.org.uk**.

'And let us consider how we may spur one another on toward love and good deeds.'

Hebrews 10:24

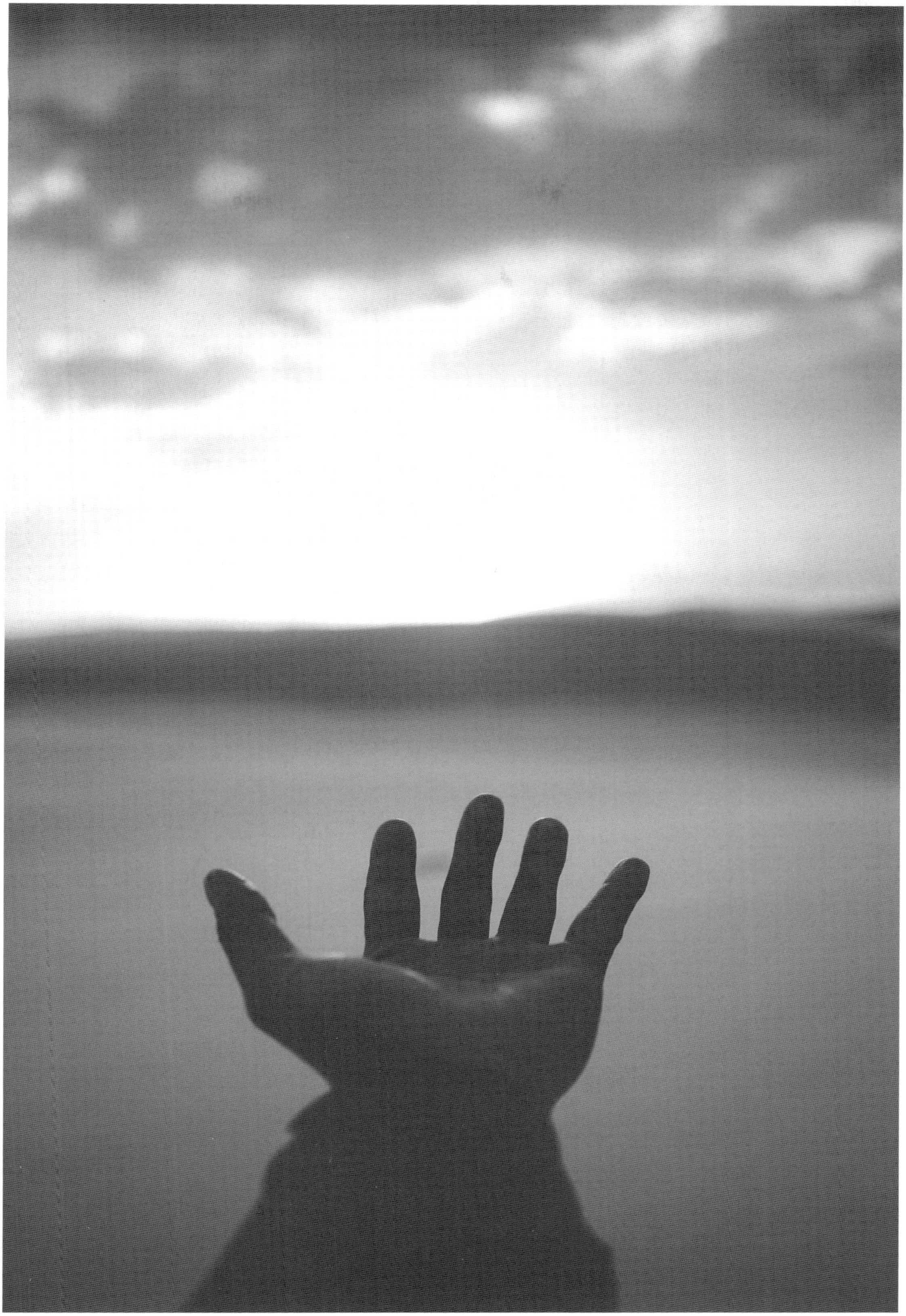

TIME

Seeing and stewarding our time through the lens of eternity

> ❝ We can be busy and fruitful servants without being ruled by the clock and running ourselves into the ground.

Now and Forever

The Shorter Westminster Catechism, written in the middle of the seventeenth century, provides answers to 107 questions of the Christian faith. The first question and answer are often quoted: 'What is the chief end of man? To glorify God and to enjoy him forever'. If this is our main purpose, how is it reflected in our stewardship of the gift of time?

Barcelona's iconic Basilica de la Sagrada Familia is a church under construction. Visitors to the site can witness the different phases of the building work, which has been ongoing since the foundation stone was laid over 140 years ago. Within the same city is the gothic Cathedral of Barcelona, work on which began in 1298 and continued for a staggering 615 years, concluding in 1913. What faith the builders must have had to believe that the time and effort put in would be worthwhile in the end, whenever that might be! Whilst most of the workers would not live to see the completion of these churches, they surely had some sense of their time being well-used, of being part of a significant undertaking and of the greater purpose: to create a sacred space for people to glorify and enjoy God for centuries to come.

It's difficult to imagine working on such a long-term project, particularly within our culture of daily targets and instant gratification. Taking the long view is challenging when 'time is money' and every minute has to be justified – both to others and to ourselves. We are inclined to focus on today's tasks, this week's commitments and, if pushed, plans for the year ahead.

We talk of wasting time, spending time, being short of time, pushed for time and time-pressured. Contrast this with how time is presented in Scripture. Ecclesiastes 3:1 reminds us that 'there is a time for everything, and a season for every activity under the heavens', and in verse 11, 'God has made everything beautiful in its time' and has 'set eternity in the human heart'.

Eternity may seem far removed from our day-to-day existence, but God has put some sense of 'forever' into our hearts so that we might grasp that our time here is just the beginning of our story. C S Lewis touched on this when he reflected 'if we find ourselves with a desire that nothing in this world can satisfy, the most probable explanation is that we were made for another world'.[3]

The promise of eternal life is at the heart of our faith, but how does 'forever' impact our stewardship of time in the here and now? If our chief purpose is to glorify and enjoy God forever, how might that start in the present, rather than be shelved for the next life?

To be effective and joyful stewards, maintaining an eternal perspective, we must be intentional about how we use our time, encompassing Sabbath, service and spontaneity.

By setting aside a proportion of our time each week for worship and resting in God – often referred to as Sabbath – we prioritise God and commit to deepening our relationship with the divine. This develops in us a perspective which is informed by the eternal values of God's kingdom.

This viewpoint helps us measure the true worth of the things we do with our time and how we serve God. We can't side-step our commitments, nor should we, but we can seek to introduce balance, adopt healthier rhythms and practices, and be kinder to ourselves. We can be busy and fruitful servants without being ruled by the clock and running ourselves into the ground. God can guide us towards fullness of life which isn't measured by diary entries.

The notion of being intentionally spontaneous may seem contradictory, but how many of us are so constrained by our diaries that there is no opportunity to step off the treadmill? An eternal perspective could free us up to spend time with the unexpected visitors, to make the most of that sunny day, or to take a decent break after a hard week. Work and routine are good for us, but not to the point of excluding opportunities for refreshment, recovery and joy.

Similarly, the annoying interruptions that divert us from our carefully planned schedules may not be welcome, but these can be the times when God presents new opportunities to work through us. Have you ever reflected back on a day that didn't go to plan and realised you'd been in the right place at the right time after all? Obstacles became opportunities and barriers turned into blessings.

Proverbs 16:3 says 'commit to the Lord whatever you do, and he will establish your plans', and verse 9 says 'in their hearts humans plan their course, but the Lord establishes their steps'. We place our time into God's hands, trusting that we will be led to value, use and enjoy this extraordinary and eternal gift for God's glory.

THINK/SHARE:

Tell someone or make a note of a time when:

- you benefited from being spontaneous
- you spent your time wisely and why you felt it was valuable
- your faith informed how you spent your time
- you were conscious of taking time to enjoy God.

REFLECT:

Reflect on your own experiences or the stories you have heard from others on this theme. Now read Ephesians 5:8-20.

Consider:

- how living as 'children of light' might lead to a full and abundant life
- how you might better understand God's will for your life
- whether God might be prompting you to review and change your routine.

'Be very careful, then, how you live – not as unwise but as wise, making the most of every opportunity, because the days are evil. Therefore do not be foolish, but understand what the Lord's will is.' (Eph. 5:15-17)

ACT:

Having reflected on God's generous gift of time, how will you respond?

Consider:

- reviewing how your time is spent each week, reflecting on the value and importance of these activities
- asking God to guide your thinking and your planning around your use of time
- being kinder to yourself, ensuring that you are intentional about taking time off and including activities which bring you joy
- speaking to your church leaders about how your congregation can better support people in achieving balance in relation to time for Sabbath, service and spontaneity.

RESOURCES:

Scripture:
Mark 2:23-28
Galatians 6:7-10

Books:

Dorothy C Bass, **Receiving the Day: Christian Practices for Opening the Gift of Time** (Minneapolis: Fortress Press, 2019)

Leighton Ford, **The Attentive Life: Discerning God's Presence in All Things** (Downers Grove: InterVarsity Press, 2014)

Jenny Odell, **Saving Time: Discovering a Life Beyond the Clock** (London: Bodley Head, 2023)

Jani Rubery, **Life Issues Bible Study: Time** (Farnham: CWR, 2009)

John Swinton, **Becoming Friends of Time** (London: SCM Press, 2017)

Websites:

The Sabbath Practice – **practicingtheway.org/sabbath**

Thy Kingdom Come – **thykingdomcome.global**

Case Study

Time for Reflection

Rev David C Cameron

Our relationship with time is influenced by many things and it changes as we move through the different seasons of life. Rev David Cameron has been reflecting back on thirty years of ministry, following his move into retirement in early 2023:

As I approached the time to leave my last parish of Dalmeny and Queensferry, I accepted an invitation to speak at a conference on the topic: 'What would I do differently?' This presentation required me to actively review how I'd spent my time and what my priorities had been over the course of my ministry. I was forced to consider whether I would make those same choices again – with the benefit of hindsight – and whether I'd always achieved the right balance.

As David prepared his talk, he reflected on the ministry of Jesus, who, it seems, developed a balance: prioritising time with God, often in solitude; time with the disciples, individually and collectively; time with the 'congregation' of workers and followers; and time with the wider community.

Looking back, I guess I would like to have achieved something of the balance in relationships that Jesus models. Time is finite when you are in a busy job with competing demands, but relationships have to be the most important investment of our time.

In the course of David's ministry, there was no such thing as a typical day. Each was varied and, to a degree, unpredictable. He became aware of the need to plan ahead and build in time for renewal.

Keeping all of the plates spinning was always a challenge; sometimes they wobbled and fell completely. I had to learn to take time to prepare for certain tasks and to give myself space to recover from the more demanding aspects of the role. I would reserve a day each month for personal reflection, often going away to a retreat centre to stop, connect and be still in the presence of the One who called me. I learned to trust that God's timing, rather than my schedule, was perfect.

In his talk, David referenced Ephesians 4, drawing out the different features of a life in ministry and the journey towards spiritual maturity:

So Christ himself gave the apostles, the prophets, the evangelists, the pastors and teachers, to equip his people for works of service, so that the body of Christ may be built up until we all reach unity in the faith and in the knowledge of the Son of God and become mature, attaining to the whole measure of the fullness of Christ. (Eph. 4:11-13)

This sense of being equipped for service, building up, progressing towards unity and experiencing the fullness of Christ provides a benchmark for how we use our time. Those verses also remind us that no-one embodies all of the vital ministries. We need each other, so that, together, we might reach unity and maturity – and avoid burning out and struggling to be what we are not!

He concludes, 'I would encourage every follower of Jesus to take time out on a regular basis for an intentional review of their day-to-day lives with that bigger picture in mind'.

> **"I learned to trust that God's timing, rather than my schedule, was perfect.**

VOLUNTEERS

Serving one another to further God's work in the world

> ❝ When we volunteer, we grow in our faith in a number of ways.

Christianity with its Sleeves Rolled Up

Do you volunteer? Maybe you are a Scout leader or work at an animal shelter. Perhaps you serve tea and coffee at a church or read scripture during services. You might even pick up groceries for a neighbour or call people who are housebound.

Volunteering is an act of generosity. When we volunteer, we choose to dedicate the finite resources of time, energy and skills to help other people. We may choose to volunteer because we are passionate about an issue, because we want to connect with other people or because it makes us happier and gives us a sense of purpose.

For Christians, though, volunteering isn't just a nice thing that we choose to do - it's an essential part of our discipleship. We are called as disciples to live out our faith in God's power to transform lives by working together to make the world a better place. The word 'volunteering' doesn't appear in the Bible, but the words 'service' and 'good works' appear all the time! In Mark, Jesus says, 'For even the Son of Man did not come to be served, but to serve, and to give his life as a ransom for many' (Mark 10:45). Throughout the New Testament, we read that it's our role as Christians to live out our faith by serving one another (Luke 8:1-3; Luke 22:26-27; Acts 9:36-39; Gal. 6:10).

The book of James is very clear that faith without action is meaningless:

> Suppose a brother or a sister is without clothes and daily food. If one of you says to them, 'Go in peace; keep warm and well fed,' but does nothing about their physical needs, what good is it? In the same way, faith by itself, if it is not accompanied by action, is dead. (James 2:15-17)

Service, therefore, is a vital expression of our life as disciples. Jesus performed the ultimate act of service by dying for the world, and so we are called to return that service by loving one another through action and deed, as he loved us (Eph. 2:10).

When we volunteer, we grow in our faith in a number of ways. We learn to discern our own gifts and how we can use those gifts to help others; we learn to work with other people to build the kingdom of God; and we learn to recognise gifts and skills in other people - both the people we work alongside and the people we serve. We develop a sense of belonging, and we learn to find fulfilment and joy in serving God.

But what does it mean to be a good steward in the context of volunteering? On an individual level, we can prayerfully discern how we can best use our finite time and our gifts to serve God and each other. We can strive to grow in our skills and our faith – in effect, investing our energy in becoming better servants and disciples. We can share the love of God, particularly with those who have no faith: we do this by demonstrating God's love through our actions and attitudes. We can seek always to be 'salt and light to the world' (Matt. 5:13-16), making sure that our faith has a positive impact on everyone around us. We act as 'salt and light', not only through our volunteering within the church, but through our service in the world at large. Our roles as volunteers for non-church organisations – whether that be at a foodbank, a nursing home, the RNLI or anywhere else – bring glory to God.

As the collective body of the church, though, it is essential for us to think also about how we can be wise stewards of our volunteers. Every church needs volunteers in order to run: people who help lead worship, people who welcome visitors, people who maintain and repair the church building, people who work with children and people who advance mission and outreach. If we're not careful, we can end up taking all of the people who do these essential tasks for granted. It is important to thank people for their service, ensure that we don't overburden individuals, and give people opportunities for growth and development in the life of the church. We have the opportunity to discern the gifts of individuals in the congregation and invite them into a deeper life of service within the church. We can make sure that everyone has an opportunity to serve, even just by asking someone to help tidy up after a service or hand out notice sheets. And we can foster a culture of gratitude, where not just the leaders but all in our church community recognise and appreciate one another's mutual service.

As both individuals and as the body of Christ, we are called to demonstrate our love for one another through our service. As disciples, we practice generosity by serving other people as Christ served us.

THINK/SHARE:

Tell someone or make a note about:
- a time when you have made a difference by volunteering, either within or outwith your church
- a time when someone has helped or supported you through volunteering
- a time when volunteers have had a positive impact in your congregation.

REFLECT:

Reflect on your own experiences or the stories you have heard from others on this theme. Now read 1 John 3:16-18; 22-24.

Consider:
- how volunteering is an expression of faith or a way of 'laying down our lives for our brothers and sisters' (v. 16)
- what it means to 'love not with word or speech, but with actions and in truth' (v. 18)
- how your church currently relates to and supports its volunteers.

'Dear children, let us not love with words or speech but with actions and in truth.'
(1 John 3:18)

ACT:

Having reflected on how volunteering is a way of serving God in gratitude, how will you respond?

Consider:
- volunteering to support a project or cause about which you are passionate
- thanking a volunteer who has served you or your church
- promoting new opportunities for service at your church, and encouraging others to volunteer.

RESOURCES:

Scripture:

Matthew 25:35-40
Colossians 3:23-24

Books:

Young, Jason, and Jonathan Malm, **The Volunteer Effect: How Your Church Can Find, Train, and Keep Volunteers Who Make a Difference**. (Grand Rapids, Michigan: Baker Books, A Division of Baker Publishing Group, 2020)

Websites:

Scottish Council for Voluntary Organisations – **scvo.scot**

Volunteers' Week – **volunteersweek.org**

Case Study

From Volunteering to Belonging
The Hot Chocolate Trust

The Hot Chocolate Trust is a youth work project in Dundee. Hot Chocolate was started by the Steeple Church in 2001 and is now a community of about 400 young people and twenty-five staff and volunteers. Hot Chocolate offers drop-ins, one-on-one support, art programmes, music facilities, outdoor pursuits and more.

At the core of Hot Chocolate's work is an emphasis on youth ownership. Traditional models of charity work view volunteers as active agents, whose role is to help passive beneficiaries. Under that model, the charity decides what is best for its beneficiaries, and the beneficiaries simply receive whatever the charity offers. In contrast, the young people involved at Hot Chocolate play a key role in deciding the direction of the organisation's plans and activities, and the volunteers also receive opportunities to develop and grow. The Volunteer Coordinator at Hot Chocolate stated, 'We don't want to do things *to* young people. We don't want to do things *for* young people. We want to do things *with* young people'.

This ownership starts with Hot Chocolate's core offering: the drop-in sessions. The young people have freedom to use the space and engage in whatever activities they wish. The volunteers and youth workers are simply present in the space, and the young people can engage with them as they see fit. Staff, volunteers and young people all play a part in strategic decision-making. Hot Chocolate is currently renovating its premises. The architects engaged the young people in a co-designing process to create a space that suited their needs. A young person also serves on the recruitment panel for new staff members. The Coordinator stated that involving the young people is a matter of balance: 'the young people bring ideas we never would have thought of, and our staff and volunteers bring ideas that they never would have thought of'.

Developing and stewarding volunteers is also key to the ethos at Hot Chocolate. Volunteers are given the same training opportunities as paid staff members. Even at the board level, great emphasis is placed on fostering a community where the humanity of everyone is recognised. Said one trustee, 'I don't think any of us at Hot Chocolate would say "I'm just a volunteer". I think they'd say "I'm part of the community at Hot Chocolate"'.

> **I see things differently now, I think about things more. It's seeping its way into all corners of my life.**

Many volunteers previously used the space as young people. As one youth work trainee said, 'I was a young person [at Hot Chocolate] for seven or eight years, and I realised I wanted to do what HC does. So, when a trainee opportunity came up, I was able to join the volunteer team to do arty youth work. I've learnt loads. I see things differently now, I think about things more. It's seeping its way into all corners of my life'.

The volunteers and staff members share a meal together before each session, and debrief after each session. Because of the collaborative culture at Hot Chocolate, volunteers aren't expected to have all the answers. Simply being available to young people is key. As one young person said, 'What really makes a difference is having people who really care, who check up, who make you feel heard and noticed'.

For more information about The Hot Chocolate Trust, visit **www.hotchocolate.org.uk**.

GIFTS

Celebrating and sharing our skills, talents, interests and passions

> " A flourishing society requires all of our different gifts and contributions.

Recognising and Releasing

What do you do that makes you feel most alive? A talent in which you are skilled, perhaps? Hobbies or interests that bring you fulfilment? Maybe it's a burning passion for a particular issue that you hold in your heart? All of these are gifts given in God's generosity.

Acts 9:36-42 tells the story of an early disciple named Tabitha, who had a gift for sewing. She used this gift to make clothing for poor widows in the community. While Tabitha's gift of sewing would certainly have been appreciated by these widows, this gift is outwardly less dramatic than other gifts we see in the book of Acts, such as proclamation, healing and speaking in tongues. It would have been easy for Tabitha's talents to be overlooked by her community, yet we see that this is not what happened. When she dies, members of the community rush to fetch Peter who visits her home. The widows who have gathered to mourn pay tribute to Tabitha by showing Peter the clothing that she had made for them. Tabitha is the only woman in the New Testament to be explicitly referred to as a disciple, and she is called this because of how she uses her gift for sewing. Her skills, her compassion and her love for others inspired the community around her and served as a testament to Christ's love.

Tabitha's story is a reminder that God has blessed us with a variety of gifts that are all equally valuable in the building up of God's kingdom. No gift is less important than any other – all are essential to the functioning of the whole. Archbishop Desmond Tutu puts it this way:

> Have you seen a symphony orchestra? They are all dolled up and beautiful with their magnificent instruments, cellos, violins etc. Sometimes there is a chap at the back carrying a triangle. Now and again the conductor will point to him and he will play 'ting'. That might seem so insignificant, but in the conception of the composer, something irreplaceable would be lost to the total beauty of the symphony if that 'ting' did not happen.[4]

This sense of everyone playing their part applies to society as a whole and to the church in particular. A flourishing society requires all of our different gifts and contributions. The same is true in our churches. Within our congregations there are people who exercise their gifts in worship, prayer, administration, care of the buildings and grounds, offering hospitality, working with different generations, volunteering for community projects, speaking out for justice, challenging the status quo, comforting the hurting, fundraising, bringing people to church, and much more besides. Whether our part feels large or small, whether we value what we have to offer or not, our own skills, gifts and personality offer a unique contribution towards the life of the whole church community and are pleasing to God.

Our gifts – whatever they may be – are given to us by God. Living generously means offering our gifts back to God in service, both within the church and in other areas of our lives. We are privileged to be called to use our gifts for the benefit of others and for the glory of God. Exercising our God-given gifts is life-giving, joyful and fulfilling. More than this, using our gifts can inspire others to release their own gifts. We see this in that same story from Acts, where Tabitha's use of her gifts inspires action and ignites gifts in other people, even after her death. The women in her community exercise the gift of compassion when they wash and dress her body. The men in her community exercise the gift of practical action when they go to fetch Peter who uses his gifts to raise Tabitha from death. All of these gifts show the power of Christ's love to more and more people.

Recognising that all people are bestowed with gifts by God means that everyone we encounter, in whatever situation, has a gift to offer and to celebrate. Many people find it hard to recognise that they have any gifts to offer, so we can ask God to help us discern gifts in both ourselves and others. We can then encourage others to exercise their gifts and when they do, we become witnesses to the work of the Holy Spirit within them.

This then opens up a way of discerning what God might be calling our church community to do. Rather than coming up with ideas for what the church ought to be doing and then struggling to find people to fill the necessary roles, an alternative starting point is to ask what gifts God has provided and therefore what God might be calling us to do. This shifts our focus from the institutional needs of the church to the power of the Holy Spirit working within us, and that is a gift indeed!

THINK/SHARE:

Tell someone or make a note of a time when:

- you have been blessed or helped through another person's gifts
- something prevented you from making the most of your gifts
- someone encouraged or enabled you to use a gift.

REFLECT:

Reflect on your own experiences or the stories you have heard from others on this theme. Now read Ephesians 4:7-13.

Consider:

- in what ways God has equipped you for service
- how you could use your gifts to the glory of God at home, in your school/workplace, at church or in other areas of life
- how you can encourage and help release the gifts of others.

'Each one of us has received a special gift in proportion to what Christ has given.' (Eph. 4:7 GNT)

ACT:

Having reflected on God's generosity in the area of gifts, how will you respond?

Consider:
- expressing gratitude to God for the diversity of gifts we encounter
- committing to enjoying your gifts in a new way
- encouraging someone else in the use of their gifts
- evaluating the gifts of your church community and reflecting on how God might be calling your congregation to use these.

RESOURCES:

Scripture:
Romans 12:3-13
1 Peter 4:7-11

Books:
Francis Dewar, **Live for a Change: Discovering and Using Your Gifts** (London: Darton, Longman and Todd, 1988)

Mark Yaconelli, **Disappointment, Doubt and Other Spiritual Gifts** (London: SPCK, 2016)

Martin Kitchen, **A Talent for Living: Reflecting on Faith and Its Fruits** (London: SPCK, 2003)

Websites:
Cinnamon Network - **cinnamonconnect.co.uk**

Case Study

A Gifted and Contributing Community

Grassmarket Community Project, Greyfriars Kirk, Edinburgh

Greyfriars Kirk, a 400-year-old congregation located in Edinburgh's Grassmarket, serves as an example of the transformative impact that can be achieved by recognising and utilising people's gifts. Historically, the Grassmarket neighbourhood experienced high deprivation and had a significant unhoused population. Over the centuries, Greyfriars Kirk had undertaken various mission projects, including a medical apothecary for the poor and a soup kitchen, both of which served as vital support for Edinburgh's most vulnerable residents. However, in 2010, the congregation embarked on a new approach to service which emphasised journeying alongside people and recognising the value they had to offer.

Rev Dr Richard Frazer, the parish minister, recognised that conventional approaches to charity often unintentionally create a divide between 'the helpers' and 'the helped'. Such models create the illusion that the helpers possess all the answers and solutions for the lives of the helped. To challenge this, Greyfriars adopted more inclusive language, referring to everyone involved in the projects as 'members' rather than volunteers or service users. This subtle shift signalled a profound change in perspective and set the stage for a transformative journey where all members' gifts were recognised and valued.

One of the earliest projects embodying this new ethos was Grassmarket Furniture. Many individuals who frequented the soup kitchen had expressed interest in woodworking, so Richard connected with a former carpenter who volunteered to teach woodworking classes. Using recycled church pews, participants not only learned woodworking skills but also witnessed their own growth and new-found confidence. This initiative became a testament to the untapped potential residing within individuals who may face homelessness or vulnerability but who possess remarkable gifts waiting to be unleashed.

Inspired by the success of Grassmarket Furniture, the Grassmarket umbrella expanded to encompass a diverse range of projects. Members gifted in weaving and sewing crafted Grassmarket tartans, forming a textile project that beautifully represented their talents, producing quality gifts appealing to the tourist market. Cooking classes were introduced to enhance members' confidence and nutritional knowledge, eventually blossoming into a thriving catering business. Individuals with green fingers cultivated a herb garden, and classes on various subjects, including art, drama and hill-walking, were led by members. Several of these initiatives evolved into social enterprises, enabling members to utilise their gifts to support the project financially. This reciprocal relationship allowed members to move beyond being solely recipients of support, to contributing actively to the project's success.

> "The remarkable success... stems from the recognition and cultivation of the diverse gifts possessed by everyone involved.

The remarkable success of Greyfriars' approach stems from the recognition and cultivation of the diverse gifts possessed by everyone involved. It is a testament to the initial vision of the congregation, the skills of members who teach classes or spearhead initiatives, and the talents of individuals who contribute through grant-writing or serving as trustees. Collectively, these gifts bear witness to the transformative power of Christ's love and embody the essence of the congregation's mission.

The journey undertaken by Greyfriars Kirk in harnessing the power of people's gifts demonstrates the immense potential that lies within communities of faith and within each individual we encounter in our communities. By moving beyond traditional charity models and embracing a more inclusive and empowering approach, Greyfriars has created a thriving community where the Holy Spirit is at work and where gifts are unleashed, uplifted, utilised and celebrated.

MONEY

Adopting a generous and intentional attitude to money

> **Acknowledging that everything we have comes from God frees us from the burden of money and the insatiable hunger for more.**

Your Money Where Your Heart Is

The Bible has a lot to say about money. Scripture contains around 2,300 verses on the subject, and at least eleven of Jesus' parables make mention of it. Why is money such a recurrent and important theme, and why was Jesus so focussed on challenging people's attitudes to it?

According to an old saying, money should never be discussed in polite company. Yet whether or not we realise it, the topic of money is often present in our conversations. We talk of holidays booked, charities supported, birthdays celebrated, bodies pampered, clubs joined, wardrobes refreshed and bargains found. Even in more straitened circumstances, we refer to 'tightening our belts', 'shopping around' or 'cutting our coat according to our cloth'. The word 'money' may not always be used directly, but it's there, front and centre. Money really does talk!

Global inequalities, as well as cultural backgrounds and personal circumstances, will have a bearing on how we relate to money. Around 10% of the world's population owns 76% of the wealth and receives 52% of the income,[5] resulting in very privileged lives for some, and very impoverished circumstances for many.

Whether you regard yourself as being either rich or poor, or somewhere in-between, Scripture makes it clear that there is a direct link between our treasure and our heart.

One of the money-related parables of Jesus, found in Luke 18:9-14, depicts a Pharisee and a tax collector praying in the temple. The Pharisee's prayer goes like this: 'God, I thank you that I am not like other people – robbers, evildoers, adulterers – or even like this tax collector. I fast twice a week and give a tenth of all I get.'

In stark contrast, the tax collector's words express deep humility, praying: 'God, have mercy on me, a sinner'.

Jesus sums up this story by highlighting that it was the tax collector who went home 'justified before God' – in other words 'made right'.

For those listening to that parable at the time, it's possible their preconceptions about the Pharisee and the tax collector led them to anticipate a different ending: one where the religious figure was praised for his pious acts of fasting and tithing, and the tax-man berated for his sins.

Those may be understandable conclusions to reach, based on cultural assumptions and prejudices. Jesus, however, honed in on what was in the hearts of the two men as they prayed in the temple: one man very sure of himself, his reputation and law-honouring habits; the other seeking mercy, conscious only of his need for God's grace and forgiveness.

This parable illustrates that God isn't impressed with bluster, hollow rituals and grandstanding, but is honoured when we draw near with humility and authenticity. When we have a deep, heartfelt recognition of God's indescribable love and undeserved grace towards us, we are compelled to respond. This is how we live out our faith.

Adopting the values of God's kingdom helps us to look beyond our own needs and towards the needs of others, to actively work for a fairer society and a spread of resources for our neighbours, wherever and whoever they might be.

What we do with the money we have reflects what is in our hearts. When our lives are God-centred, our giving to God will be generous, joyful and meaningful. It will be costly and require us to adjust our own perceived needs and wants. Acknowledging that everything we have comes from God frees us from the burden of money and the insatiable hunger for more.

Many people of faith choose to give a proportion of their regular income to God – making this the first thing they do with their income each week or month. These first offerings to God are an important part of being church, and so this giving is usually directed through our own congregation, enabling the church in every place to minister and serve. It's not a subscription or a payment towards the running costs. Rather, this giving is an important part of our personal and public worship, as we join with other believers to express thankfulness and contribute to God's work.

Our monetary giving to God may begin with the church offering, but it doesn't end there. How we steward the remaining portion is also an expression of our worship and faith. Our thankfulness to God should result in generosity in every aspect of our lives, reflecting the love of Jesus to others and bringing glory to God.

THINK/SHARE:

Tell someone or make a note of a time when:

- you or your community benefitted from someone else's generosity
- you felt led to give spontaneously to a cause or situation and why
- you were impacted by the significant poverty or wealth in your own or another community and how it made you feel.

REFLECT:

Reflect on your own experiences or the stories you have heard from others on this theme. Now read 2 Corinthians 9:6-15.

Consider:

- where giving to God sits within your priorities
- if, and how, joy and generosity are connected in your life
- how your faith has influenced your spending habits.

'Each of you should give what you have decided in your heart to give, not reluctantly or under compulsion, for God loves a cheerful giver.' (2 Cor. 9:7)

ACT:

Having reflected on God's generosity in the area of money, how will you respond?

Consider:

- reviewing your giving to God on a regular basis
- praying about any changes you need to make in your spending habits
- finding new ways to challenge financial injustice or show generosity to those most in need.

RESOURCES:

Scripture:

1 Chronicles 29:1-20
Isaiah 58
Matthew 25:14-30
Luke 21:1-4
1 Corinthians 16:1-2
1 Timothy 6:17-19

Books:

John Preston, **The Money Revolution** (Milton Keynes: Authentic Media, 2007)

Keith Tondeur and Steve Pierce, **Your Money and Your Life** (London: SPCK Publishing, 2010)

William Barclay, **Insights: Money** (Edinburgh: Saint Andrew Press, 2009)

Graham Beynon, **Money Counts** (Epsom: The Good Book Company, 2016)

Hansruedi Graf, **The Christian and Money** (London: Chapter Two, 2015)

Websites:

Christians Against Poverty (CAP) – **capuk.org**

Church of Scotland Stewardship – **churchofscotland.org.uk/resources/stewardship**

Stewardship – **stewardship.org.uk**

Case Study

Financial Accountability in Practice

The Iona Community

Members of the Iona Community account to one another for living and keeping the Community's Rule of Life. This accountability, which is practiced through 'family groups', involves deep and honest sharing about all aspects of life including how members use their money, time and Earth's resources.

Within the context of a society where poverty and wealth are revealed in so many different ways, and yet where personal money matters are rarely discussed, what does it mean to be accountable for our money?

Former Iona Community Leader, Rev John Harvey, and his wife Molly have been members of the Community for over fifty years:

> We account in detail to each other in small groups using a process which enables us each to identify our net income, once agreed expenditures are subtracted. Then we allocate, in agreement with each other, up to 10% of our disposable income, a portion of which goes to the Iona Community. A further portion is allocated to charities and causes of our choice. This is very much like a traditional tithing process. For us, this is part of our ongoing commitment to think carefully and regularly about the use of the remaining 90% of our income, keeping detailed accounts each week of all income and expenditure.

Community Leader, Rev Ruth Harvey, recognises that for some people, sharing in this way is unusual and extremely challenging. For others, it becomes easier over time:

> We may ask questions to help the accounting member come to their own clarity. It is not our role as listeners to judge or even to advise. Our role is to listen and to support the accounting member to own their decisions and to commit to a close reflection in future decision-making.

John and Molly find it a liberating experience:

> Knowing what is coming in and going out, where it's coming from and where it's going to, and sharing that information with co-members, both challenges us, and can also free us from undue anxiety about money – as the Gospel encourages us to expect!

Richard Sharples is a long-time Community member and Methodist minister. He acknowledges that financial accountability involves honesty and vulnerability:

> It requires us to literally 'put our money where our mouth is'. In over twenty years of accounting in this way within family groups, I have found it to be a means of grace; a practice which enables me to grow in holiness, which within the Methodist tradition was always 'social holiness'. For me the essence lies in the reviewing and preparation of some form of household accounts for the year, and in the discipline of laying this before others – not for them to require more from us, but to gently and lovingly receive it.

This accountability also applies to the collective Community, which takes seriously its responsibility for the use of its money in the world. This affects how much guests are asked to pay to stay at the Community's centres to ensure ease of access to those least able to pay. It also impacts how much is paid to staff, and how diligently and ethically it accounts for the use of the money entrusted to the whole Community.

> "Knowing what is coming in and going out, where it's coming from and where it's going to... both challenges us, and can also free us from undue anxiety about money..."

For more information on the Iona Community visit **www.iona.org.uk**.

POSSESSIONS

Sharing more generously of ourselves and our possessions

> ❝ The question, therefore, isn't whether or not to own things; instead, it's a question of how we relate to and use our possessions.

Trusting God Over Stuff

We live in a culture that tells us that we need more and more stuff to have a perfect life. We are bombarded by advertisements promising that products can grant us acceptance, success or happiness, yet we know in our hearts that possessions can't fulfil our deepest longings.

When we look to our possessions to grant us the love that only comes from God, the result is anxiety, selfishness and discontent. We recognise, however, that possessions aren't all bad. The joy of a child when they receive a longed-for gift, the excitement of friends gathered to celebrate a new home, the relief of a person in need when they receive a warm coat: all of these testify that possessions can contribute towards connection, security and purpose.

Scriptural teaching on possessions can seem contradictory. In Matthew 9:21, for example, Jesus commands a rich young man to 'sell all your possessions and give to the poor'. In contrast, Ecclesiastes 5:19 says that 'If God gives us wealth and property and lets us enjoy them, we should be grateful and enjoy what we have worked for. It is a gift from God.' So, which is it? Should we seek to give up all our worldly goods or should we seek to enjoy the good things we possess?

The truth is that possessions themselves are not bad or good. Possessions are just things, devoid of meaning outside that which we give them. The question, therefore, isn't whether or not to own things; instead, it's a question of how we relate to and use our possessions.

Do we see our possessions as gifts from God and respond with gratitude, or do we instead hold up our houses, cars and clothes as proof of our superiority? Do we realise that our true identity and purpose lie in God, or do we instead behave as though our ultimate aim in this world is to acquire more things? Do we seek to share and use the things we have to further God's kingdom, or do we instead hold tightly onto what we have because we think that our possessions keep us secure?

The parable of the rich fool in Luke 12 illustrates what it looks like to have the wrong attitude towards possessions. Jesus tells the listening crowd the story of a rich farmer who had an abundant harvest. Faced with more grain than he could ever use, the farmer decides to tear down his barns and build bigger ones, enabling him to stockpile several years' worth of grain. But God responds to the unsuspecting farmer with these frank words: 'You fool! This very night your life will be demanded from you. Then who will get what you have prepared for yourself?'

This parable may fill us with anxiety. It may seem like Jesus is critiquing *all* possessions, but this is not the case. Jesus isn't saying that it was wrong for the man to plan for the future, but is instead challenging the man's overarching attitude towards his possessions.

The farmer placed his trust in his possessions, believing that they were capable of keeping him safe and secure. He chose to keep more possessions than he could ever possibly use, concerned about his own wellbeing, rather than thinking of his family, farmhands or neighbours. Like the farmer, we too may want to believe that the more stuff we have, the safer we are. We forget that this security is an illusion: all material things waste away or can be destroyed. No amount of 'stuff' can protect us: this is the sobering truth of our mortality.

But the good news is that our future in God is secure. We don't need to justify ourselves through our belongings or reinvent our identities through the things we own. Our identity, purpose and security are in the Living God. By placing our trust in God, we can invest in things that are everlasting – our walk of faith and our relationship with Christ – living lives that are 'rich towards God' (Luke 12:21).

While it is not realistic for us to get rid of everything we own, we can reflect on whether our attitudes towards our possessions keep us from a closer relationship with God. We can discern how we might share more generously. We can seek to consume more mindfully. We can campaign for legislative change against corporations that create harmful products or items that cannot easily be repaired or recycled. We can seek opportunities to share, re-use and lend. We can take care of the things we have and reduce the amount of waste we produce. We can dispose of things in a way that reduces harm, by donating or recycling.

Everything we have comes from God, who calls us to place our hope in eternal promises, not earthly possessions: 'Provide purses for yourselves that will not wear out, a treasure in heaven that will never fail, where no thief comes near and no moth destroys. For where your treasure is, there your heart will be also.' (Luke 12:33b-34)

THINK/SHARE:

Tell someone or make a note of a time when:

- you felt affected by consumerism
- you gave something away for the benefit of yourself or others
- your congregation used its possessions to benefit the wider community.

REFLECT:

Reflect on your own experiences or the stories you have heard from others on this theme. Now read Matthew 6:19-21.

Consider:

- where you tend to place your trust
- what it looks like to store up 'treasures in heaven'
- whether there are resources needed to help your congregation better serve its community.

'Where your treasure is, there your heart will be also.'
(Matt. 6:21)

ACT:

Having reflected on God's generosity in the area of possessions, how will you respond?

Consider:

- praying for God's help to consume more mindfully
- finding a way to mend or reuse an item, rather than throwing it away
- searching for opportunities to borrow, share or lend items
- reviewing your church's possessions and evaluating their usefulness.

RESOURCES:

Scripture:
Luke 12:1-48
Proverbs 11:28
Matthew 16:24-26

Books:

Luke Timothy Johnson, **Sharing Possessions: What Faith Demands** (Grand Rapids: Eerdmans, 2011)

Church of Scotland Youth, **The COSY Guide to Ethical Living** (Edinburgh: Church of Scotland, 2013) - issuu.com/cofsyouth/docs/cosy_guide_to_ethical_living

Wesley K. Willmer, **God & Your Stuff** (Colorado Springs: NavPress, 2002)

Websites:

Zero Waste Scotland - **zerowastescotland.org.uk/citizens**

Case Study

An Inheritance of Blessing

Oisean a' Chalman, Uig

In the corner of the grounds of Uig Parish Church on the shores of Loch Miabhaig on the Isle of Lewis sits a small metal storehouse which makes a big difference to families across the Western Isles. This is the base of Oisean a' Chalman Banca Paisde or 'Dove's Corner Baby Bank', a project started by the congregation in late 2019.

The project invites people to donate new and pre-loved items which will be useful to new parents, such as baby and children's clothing, baby carriers, prams and buggies in addition to consumable items such as wipes, nappies and toiletries. These are then distributed to families as required on a confidential basis.

Originally established to support the communities of Uig and Bernera, the project has established a good working relationship with local health and education services and now serves the whole of the Western Isles. With support from the local authority Comhairle nan Eilean Siar and the Corra Foundation, it has also grown to provide for refugees and adults seeking special assistance, in addition to the babies, children and families. They have developed a close relationship with the Co-op, whose car park in Stornoway provides the location for goods to be donated, and who transports these goods to the Oisean a' Chalman storehouse.

As well as donating material goods, members and friends of the congregation have been generous in supporting the project financially and with their time. Volunteers meet to sort and store donations and to launder donated clothes. Even the construction of the storehouse was down to local people offering their talents. Whether through donating goods and possessions or time and service, the baby bank offers a way for one generation to support another. Rev Hugh Maurice Stewart, minister of Lochs-in-Bernera linked with Uig, explains that 'donations are an inheritance of blessing to the next generation in the Lord's name'.

As well as ensuring pre-loved possessions are given a new home, the baby bank helps restore dignity by providing what a young family needs at a time that can be challenging both emotionally and financially. The congregation tries to ensure that items distributed are of good quality, giving of the best possible.

> **Volunteers meet to sort and store donations and to launder donated clothes.**

For the congregation, this project is as spiritual as it is material, showing that God is faithful not just in times of prosperity but also in times of challenge. The baby bank offers a way of living out the Great Commandment to love God and love our neighbour and draws its inspiration from the words of Jesus in Matthew 25:40 – 'Whatever you did for one of the least of these brothers and sisters of mine, you did for me'.

Hugh has seen God at work through Oisean a' Chalman:

> The words of Isaiah 65:24 spring to mind: 'Before they call, I will answer; and while they are speaking, I will hear'. The Lord knew about the pandemic and the needs families would experience long before we did and he just loves to bless the wonderful babies, children and families through the baby bank. The intergenerational support received, both financial and in-kind, locally and across the island has been humbling and crucial to maintaining the baby bank.

EARTH

Honouring God's interconnected creation

> ❝ God is with us in our work to protect and care for the earth.

The Tapestry of Creation

God has created an awe-inspiring and interwoven universe, of which humans are blessed to be a part. We are called to recognise our place and fulfil our responsibilities in caring for creation.

In the 1990s, Professor Suzanne Simard discovered that trees in forests appear to communicate with each other through vast underground webs of fungi called mycorrhizal networks. These connected threads enable the trees across the forest to share carbon, nutrients and chemical information.[6] Through these networks, a tree under threat from disease or pests can warn other trees, and a dying tree can send its carbon to its neighbours. Trees, it turns out, are not solitary 'things' competing with other plants for resources; rather, they are part of a complex and cooperative community that allows the forest to thrive! Simard's research demonstrates that all of the earth is alive and interconnected in ways we can't even imagine—every human, plant, animal and ecosystem is interwoven in a complex tapestry of creation.

Like Simard, the Psalmists also recognised the complexity of creation: 'How many are your works, Lord! In wisdom you made them all; the earth is full of your creatures. There is the sea, vast and spacious, teeming with creatures beyond number – living things both large and small' (Psalm 104:24-25).

As Christians, we celebrate the generous abundance of God's creation: 'The whole earth is filled with awe at your wonders; where morning dawns, where evening fades, you call forth songs of joy' (Psalm 65:8). We also recognise that we are just one part of this system which is so interconnected and complex that only God can truly comprehend it.

Acknowledging the majesty of God's creation can prove challenging because doing so reveals how remiss humanity has been in its attitude toward creation. Scientific evidence overwhelmingly shows that humans have treated the world not as a complex and interconnected web of which we are a part, but as something to be controlled and used for personal gain. Humans have levelled forests, dumped pollutants into the water and atmosphere, and turned once-thriving lands to desert. Countless ecosystems have suffered due to human activity, and now humans themselves, in many parts of the world, face the brutal consequences. Those most affected are often the least responsible for creating the problems in the first place.

How can we even begin to put things right? How do we move beyond thinking that creation is something we own or control? How can we move toward renewing our planet for the benefit of all creation? For many of us, the problem feels so vast that we find ourselves paralysed, doubting that our individual actions can make any difference. Many of us feel guilt and confusion about how to change our own and humanity's behaviour.

The good news is that we don't act alone. We believe in a God of resurrection and transformation, who has the power to restore what has been broken and create new life from death. God is with us in our work to protect and care for the earth. As members of the universal church, we act together for the fulfilment of the kingdom. Transforming creation isn't an individual burden; collectively, we can impact humanity's care of creation in profound ways.

As different parts of the one body, our diverse backgrounds, contexts and passions will inform and influence our choices as to how we honour creation. For some of us, that might mean planting native plants in our gardens or making meals that utilise local and seasonal ingredients. It might mean reducing waste or using public transport. It might be prioritising sustainable fishing and agricultural practices, or investing in ethical and sustainable companies. The key is to begin somewhere, trusting that each action will weave together to create a tapestry of justice and renewal.

We can take collective action in our churches and communities. We can use our prophetic voice as a church to speak out against the systems, policies and corporations most responsible for environmental degradation. We can stand in solidarity with the communities most affected by climate change. We can lead by example, choosing to divest from environmentally-harmful businesses and to implement sustainable practices. We can support climate action projects and advocate for better environmental policies. Most of all, we can pray for God's guidance to act in ways that benefit all of creation.

Like the trees connected in a forest, God has not made us to be in competition with each other for a share of Earth's resources, but has blessed us with a world so abundant that it can provide for all creatures. We are called to support one another and all of creation so that God's kingdom may thrive here on earth as in heaven.

THINK/SHARE:

Tell someone or make a note of a time when:

- you were struck by the beauty or complexity of creation
- your view changed concerning an aspect of the earth and its care
- you acted in ways to benefit the earth.

REFLECT:

Reflect on your own experiences or the stories you have heard from others on this theme. Now read Psalm 104.

Consider:

- the power and beauty of God as expressed through creation
- how God has provided abundantly for all of creation
- your place and role in this interdependent creation.

*How many are your works, Lord!
In wisdom you made them all;
the earth is full of your creatures.
(Ps. 104:24)*

ACT:

Having reflected on God's generosity in relation to creation, how will you respond?

Consider:

- listening to those most affected by climate change
- learning more about caring for the earth by engaging with environmental conservation organisations
- calculating your household or congregation's carbon footprint using an online tool
- making positive changes in your life to benefit the earth
- encouraging your church to take collective action to honour God's creation.

RESOURCES:

Scripture:

Genesis 1-2; 9:8-17
Job 38-39

Books:

Debbie Hawker, David Hawker, Jamie Hawker, **Changing the Climate: Applying the Bible in a Climate Emergency** (Bible Reading Fellowship, 2021)

Kyle Meyaard-Schaap, **Following Jesus in a Warming World: A Christian Call to Climate Action** (Downers Grove: InterVarsity Press, 2023)

John Philip Newell, **Sacred Earth, Sacred Soul: A Celtic Guide to Listening to our Souls and Saving the World** (London: William Collins, 2021)

Ruth Valerio, **L is for Lifestyle: Christian Living that Doesn't Cost the Earth** (London: InterVarsity Press, 2019)

Websites:

A Rocha – **arocha.org**

Christian Aid – **christianaid.org.uk/get-involved/campaigns**

Climate Stewards – **climatestewards.org**

Eco-Congregation Scotland – **ecocongregationscotland.org**

Case Study

Caring Together for Change

The Eco-Congregation Scotland Movement

Many denominations around the globe use the 'Five Marks of Mission'[7] to ensure that everything they do is directly concerned with furthering Christ's mission in the world. The fifth mark is 'to strive to safeguard the integrity of creation and sustain and renew the life of the earth'. Churches and people of faith in all parts of the world are grappling with how to live out this aspect of mission in a warming world.

Eco-Congregation Scotland is one example of a faith-based movement caring passionately for God's creation and working co-operatively to encourage transformational change. Rev David Coleman, Environmental Chaplain, describes its mission:

> In prayer, worship and conversation we discover what it means to care for God's creation. We put that care into action individually, locally, nationally and globally, desiring to live justly in a transformed world. And we commit ourselves to campaigning on urgent threats to the web of life in our vulnerable world.

Duffus, Spynie and Hopeman Church is one of more than 600 congregations who are part of Eco-Congregation Scotland. Situated on the Moray coast, this church is actively caring for creation across three spheres:

- **Spiritual Living: Linking environmental issues and the Christian faith**

    The congregation regularly reflects on care for creation in worship and prayer, and members are kept informed on environmental issues through regular articles in the church magazine. Forest Church in local woodland and on the beach offers an opportunity for all ages to encounter God in creation together.

- **Practical Living: Reducing environmental impact through practical action**

    The congregation encourages practical steps that individuals can take to reduce energy use and waste. They are trying to implement an environmental purchasing policy, are seeking to use energy efficiently within their church buildings, and will ensure that future building plans are environmentally-friendly. They maintain the church and manse grounds in ways that support local wildlife.

- **Global Living: Taking action on climate change in the local and global community**

    The congregation's engagement with Christian Aid, in particular, informs the members on the impact of climate change and encourages campaign actions. The congregation is also a Fairtrade church; connects with the eco work at the local primary school; and has the Girlguiding Rainbows group involved in looking after Duffus Kirk's garden.

    The congregation was awarded its first Eco-Congregation award at the end of 2014, followed by a Silver Award in early 2018. These awards mark progress in caring for God's creation, but there is still more to be done, as the Rev Jenny Adams, Parish Minister explains:

> We are now working to an Eco Action Plan which continues to encourage action on eco-issues and activities amongst the congregation and parish. We've developed an Eco policy for the congregation and church buildings, including an ethical purchasing policy. In particular, we are trying to promote the message that it is not just the action of the church that is important, but our individual actions. We are offering practical ideas and stories of good practice, and are endeavouring to lead by example, encouraging everyone to play their part in valuing and caring for God's intricate and interconnected creation.

> "In prayer, worship and conversation we discover what it means to care for God's creation.

For more information about Eco-Congregation Scotland, visit **www.ecocongregationscotland.org**.

'You are worthy,
our Lord and God,
to receive glory and
honour and power,
for you created all things,
and by your will
they were created
and have their being.'

Revelation 4:11

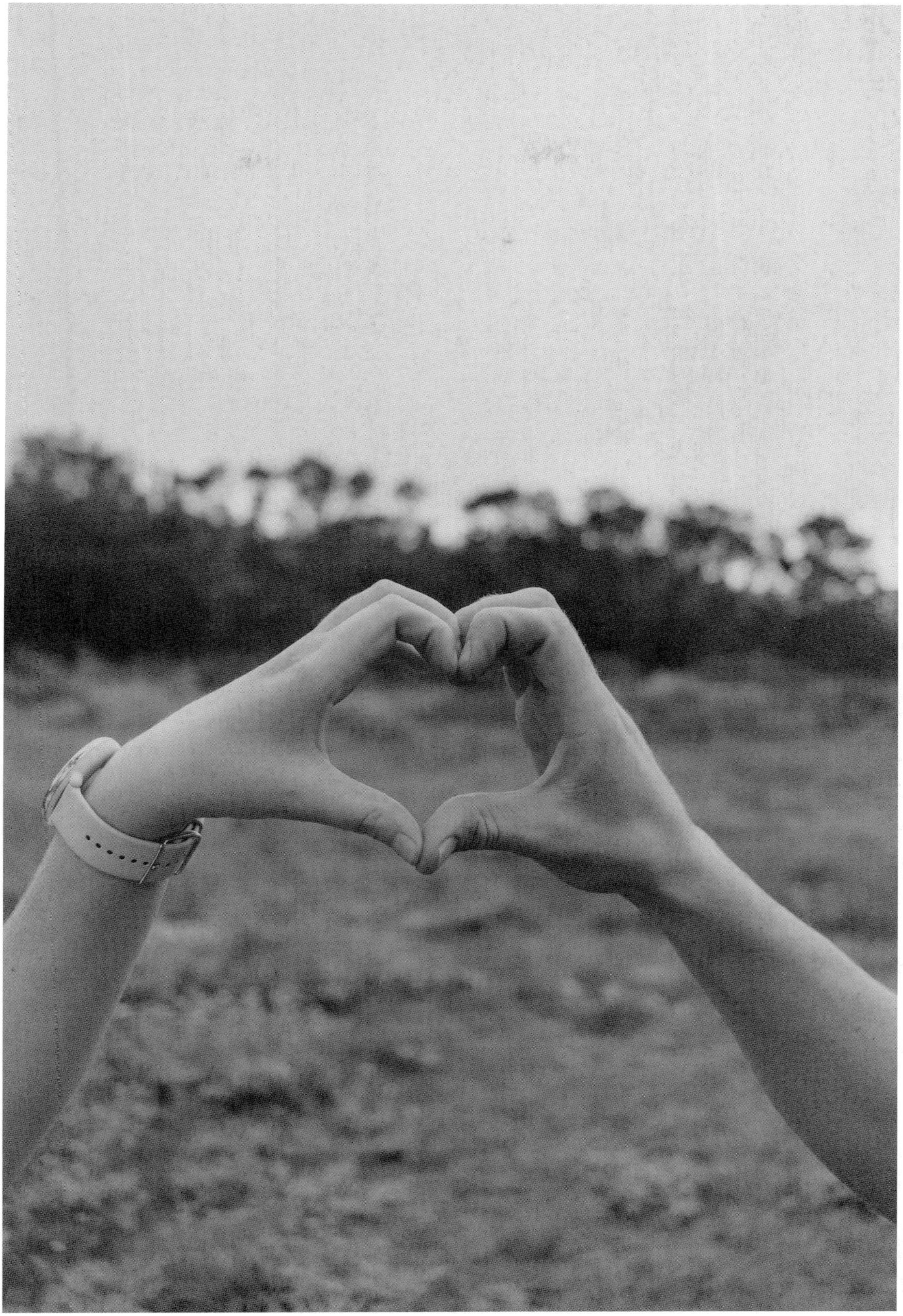

BODY

Caring for and appreciating our bodies

> **❝ Our bodies and our spirituality are inextricably linked, and have been since humanity began.**

Temples of the Holy Spirit

A human body is made up of 37.2 trillion cells. If its blood vessels were laid in a straight line, they would stretch more than twice around the world.[8] A single brain has enough data capacity to store the entire internet.[9] Our bodies truly are 'fearfully and wonderfully made' (Ps. 139:14).

Our bodies are the physical means by which we experience and interact with the world around us. It is through our bodies that we can feel the warmth of the sun, taste the sweetness of freshly picked fruit or smell the aroma of bread being baked. It is through our bodies that we can exercise creativity or sing out our song to the world.

Our bodies are a gift from God, although it may not always feel that way: as well as bringing us pleasure, bodies can also bring us pain. Bodies can be messy, achy and broken. Some people may struggle with their own or society's image of their body, while others may feel like they are in the wrong body entirely.

Christianity is an embodied faith: we believe in the Word made flesh – that God chose to come to earth as a human being, experiencing what it is to live in a physical body. Jesus, born as a human baby, knows what it was like to be dependent on and cared for by others. He knows what it's like to lose teeth, to go through puberty, to hunger and thirst, to weep, to experience physical pain. The risen Jesus appears in a broken body – wounds and all. God understands what our bodies go through not only as their Creator, but from lived experience. In many traditions, people are welcomed into our faith through the bodily act of baptism, and the bodily life of Jesus is remembered by taking bread and wine into our own bodies. Our bodies and our spirituality are inextricably linked, and have been since humanity began.

When God created human bodies, God declared them 'very good' (Gen. 1:27-31). Each body is 'wonderfully made' (Ps. 139:14). More than just physical matter, our bodies are 'temples of the Holy Spirit' (1 Cor. 3:16 and 6:19) – the very dwelling places of God. These statements are true of *all* bodies, not just those which look or function in a particular way. God created each of us to be unique, as part of a rich and diverse tapestry.

Recognising each person's uniqueness moves us to appreciate that each and every body brings blessings. Amy Kenny writes about the blessings of living in a disabled body: 'We, the disabled, know what it means to live in a way that is dependent on something other than ourselves for survival… We have a deeper sense of who God is because of our acknowledged interdependence.'[10]

Honouring one another as temples of the Holy Spirit means not expecting anyone to conform to our own ideas of what a body should be or do. This requires care around the language we use in conversation, on social media and even in our worship so as not to portray bodies or disabilities negatively. It means ensuring our spaces – including our worship spaces – are fully accessible to everyone: level access, quiet spaces, hearing loops, words printed in braille and so on.

Regardless of our outward appearance, depending on and listening to God helps guide us as we respond to God's generosity in how we use our own bodies. In the book of Daniel, the food and wine that King Nebuchadnezzar orders to be served is ritually unclean to Daniel and his friends. Daniel persuades the official to allow them to eat vegetables and drink water for ten days, after which time Daniel and his friends are noticeably healthier and stronger than those who had been eating the royal food. Making healthy choices around food and drink is one way we can honour God with our bodies. Other ways may include exercise, creativity and relaxation. We can grant ourselves rest when we are sick or weary. We can use our bodies to perform only acts of kindness, and never acts of violence. We can make time to be physically present as a comfort to the sick, hurting, lost or broken in our communities.

Evidence shows that social connection and active listening help support both physical and mental health.[11] Rachel Held Evans notes that:

> There is a difference between curing and healing, and the church is called to the slow and difficult work of healing. We are called to enter into one another's pain, anoint the sick, and stick around, no matter the outcome.[12]

Making the time to be present to someone, accepting them as they are, is an act of healing which recognises the other as wonderfully made, acknowledges God's presence within them and allows us to participate in Christ's ministry on earth. For in the words of Teresa of Avila, 'Christ has no body on earth now but yours'.

THINK/SHARE:

Tell someone or make a note of a time when:

- you have done something positive to improve your own fitness, health or wellbeing
- you have been aware of barriers to healthy living within your own community or context
- you have struggled with an aspect of your own body, and what role, if any, your faith played in dealing with that.

REFLECT:

Reflect on your own experiences or the stories you have heard from others on this theme. Now read 1 Samuel 16:1-7.

Consider:

- what can be learned from this passage about judging others by outward appearance
- how you view your own body and compare this with how God views it
- your lifestyle or daily routine and the impact this has – positively or negatively – on your wellbeing
- what opportunities or barriers to health and wellbeing exist in your community.

'The Lord does not look at the things people look at. People look at the outward appearance, but the Lord looks at the heart.' (1 Sam. 16:7b)

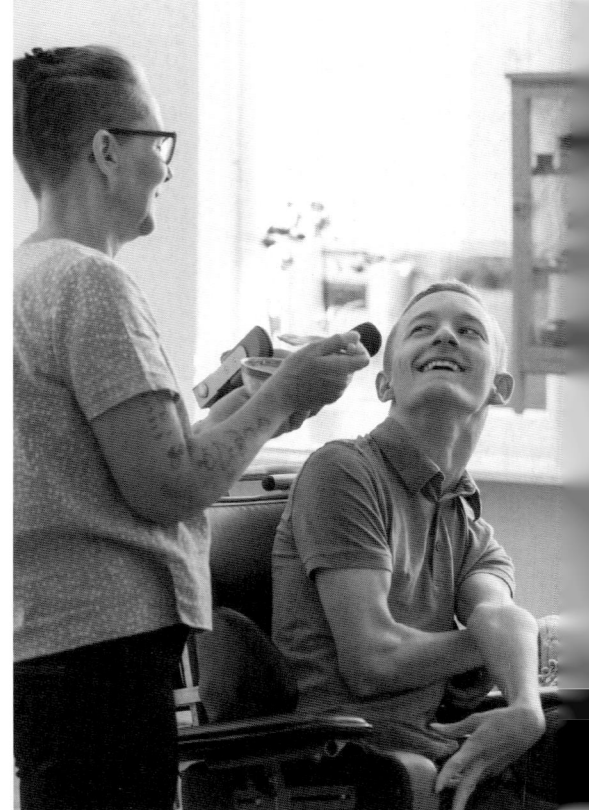

ACT:

Having reflected on God's generosity relating to bodies, how will you respond?

Consider:

- incorporating healthier activities into your personal routine
- reviewing how accessible and welcoming your space is for all
- making time to be with others, offering attentive and active listening
- celebrating the diversity of bodies God has created and the blessings each brings.

RESOURCES:

Scripture:

Romans 12:1-2
1 Corinthians 6:12-20
1 Corinthians 10:31-33

Books:

Paula Gooder, **Body: Biblical Spirituality for the Whole Person** (London: SPCK, 2016)

Amy Kenny, **My Body is Not a Prayer Request: Disability Justice in the Church** (Grand Rapids: Brazos Press, 2022)

Church of Scotland, **Diverse Gender Identities and Pastoral Care** (Edinburgh: Mission and Discipleship Council, 2018)

Websites:

Christians in Sport - **christiansinsport.org.uk**

Churches for All - **churchesforall.org.uk**

Guild of Health and St. Raphael - **gohealth.org.uk**

Kate Bowler - **katebowler.com**

Case Study

Active Faith and Active Lifestyle

Ken Reid, member of North Berwick: St Andrew Blackadder Church

From a young age, Ken Reid has enjoyed an active lifestyle. Although never particularly involved in organised sport, activities such as swimming, running, cycling and hillwalking helped him to stay fit and connect with nature. He has been part of the Scottish Christian Hillwalking Club, a group which celebrates the wonderful things God has given us by getting out and enjoying creation. By meeting on days other than a Sunday, they aim to demonstrate that an active faith and an active lifestyle can go hand-in-hand. Through activities such as this, Ken has come to realise that keeping a healthy body and mind can be a form of worship.

At the age of 26, Ken began losing his sight, but he was determined that this would not stop these activities he enjoyed. By making some adaptations, such as swimming at quieter times, counting the number of strokes in a length, and cycling on a tandem with a pilot, physical activity continues to be an important part of his life and faith. 'It helps me enjoy creation,' he says. 'Even though I can't see it, I can still appreciate being in it.'

This connection with creation helps to develop an identity and belonging in God. Ken says,

> As is appreciated by many disability groups of Christians, I am made in God's image regardless of my body – whether I'm fat or thin, tall or short, able to walk or not able to walk, black or white, male or female, sighted or blind – I am made in God's image.

He appreciates that God has blessed and enabled him to do things with his blindness, opening up opportunities for service that he would never otherwise have had.

One such opportunity was making a short film about swimming and cycling for the RNIB and British Blind Sport offering encouragement to other blind people to take up physical activity. On another occasion, he took part in a sponsored bike ride from Edinburgh to London via Belfast, Dublin and Cardiff – nearly 850 miles, with a different tandem pilot each day.

Asked how these activities have helped Ken grow in faith, he points to learning the importance of trust. 'When you get on a tandem cycle, you have to absolutely trust your pilot. On the sponsored ride, you'd wake up and get on a bike with someone you'd never met before and have to trust that they would keep you safe. I guess faith ties in with that subliminally: I always believe the best in people, and I believe that people always want the best for me.'

This same trust is needed across many areas of life: from trusting a stranger to help cross the road, to trusting the honesty of a merchant when paying with a contactless card. Ken attributes the reason he is so naturally trusting to his faith.

Speaking publicly about such activities matters to Ken: 'I want other blind people to be able to be more active, and to encourage other Christians to use their bodies. It's about enabling people to make the most of their lives.'

> "...keeping a healthy body and mind can be a form of worship.

You can view Ken's film about swimming and cycling on the RNIB website:
www.rnib.org.uk/our-campaigns/see-sport-differently/real-stories.

MIND

Being intentional and generous in the stewardship of our minds

> **"** Scientific research shows that religious practice and spirituality have a positive impact on our physical and mental health.

A Healthy and Godly Mind

In distinguishing between the brain and the mind, neuroscientist Caroline Leaf states that, 'your mind is how you, uniquely, experience life. It's responsible for how you think, feel and choose'.[13] On that basis, a whole-life approach to Christian stewardship includes consideration of the mind.

What does it mean to be a faithful steward of the mind? First, we acknowledge that the mind is an amazing gift from God. Second, we accept that this precious gift has been entrusted to our care. Given the intricacies of the mind, this duty of care may seem onerous. However, the great news is that we have direct access to the maker! We may not know the mind of God (1 Cor. 2:11), but God knows our minds (Ps. 139:1-6).

Followers of Jesus will be familiar with the value of an active devotional life, regularly taking time to connect with God. We consider our relationship with God in another chapter but, for now, we focus specifically on the benefits of spiritual practices to our minds.

Scientific research shows that religious practice and spirituality have a positive impact on our physical and mental health.[14] The evidence highlights a strong correlation between prayer and improved coping skills, general health and even longevity. Engaging in spiritual practices can ground us, calm the nervous system, reduce anger and provide many of the tools we need to live resiliently. Talking with God is good for us. The science is in line with Scripture on this. Philippians 4:6-7 urges us to bring our concerns and anxious thoughts to God in prayer, so that we might receive God's peace which guards our hearts and minds.

Having a faith provides a lens through which we can evaluate life, including its troubles and big questions. Colossians 3:1-2 says 'Since, then, you have been raised with Christ, set your hearts on things above, where Christ is, seated at the right hand of God. Set your minds on things above, not on earthly things.' Focussing our minds on the things of God influences how we see ourselves, others and the world. Our perspective shifts as the Holy Spirit helps us to reflect on everything from a divine viewpoint. The contrast between 'earthly things' and 'things above' is highlighted by Jesus in Matthew 5:3-10 where we catch a glimpse of the distinctiveness of God's kingdom. The world's values are turned upside-down. Generosity is focussed towards those who are most often last in the queue: the forgotten, the struggling, the persecuted.

How might we apply those kingdom values and that same generosity to caring for our minds?

First, we can start by being generous in how we think about ourselves. The Psalms describe our place within creation as being 'crowned with glory and honour' (Ps. 8:5) and point to a God who created us with intention: we are 'fearfully and wonderfully made' (Ps. 139:14). For followers of Jesus, our sense of self relates to who we are in Christ. Ephesians 1:3-4 says:

> Praise be to the God and Father of our Lord Jesus Christ, who has blessed us in the heavenly realms with every spiritual blessing in Christ. For he chose us in him before the creation of the world to be holy and blameless in his sight.

Take a moment here! You are blessed, you are chosen and, through Christ, you are made holy and blameless. This perspective provides us with a generous sense of who we are as children of God that is unshaken by human shortcomings or others' perceptions of us. It is neither an inflated nor a deflated sense of self. Rather, it is an acceptance of our personal worth as valued within God's economy, where love, forgiveness and grace are freely given through faith in Jesus.

Second, we can exercise generosity towards others by contributing to a culture of well-being. How often do you find that your mood is boosted when you are chatting with a friend? They may not hold a counselling qualification, but they help foster a lighter spirit within you all the same, whether by offering a listening ear, providing a diversion from spiralling thoughts or simply making you laugh. If you've been blessed by someone else's 'ministry of presence', you can offer the same to others in turn.

Third, we can exercise generosity by dedicating our intellect, thoughts, passions, creativity, humour, emotions and choices to the glory of God, following the commandment of Jesus to love God with our whole heart, soul and mind (Matt. 22:37).

THINK/SHARE:

Tell someone or make a note of a time when:
- you were engaged in an activity or project which brought you joy and fulfilment
- someone had a positive impact on your well-being
- your faith influenced your thinking about a world event or personal circumstance.

REFLECT:

Reflect on your own experiences or the stories you have heard from others on this theme. Now read Galatians 5:22-23.

Consider:
- the fruit of the Spirit, reflecting on each one in turn
- how these might relate to your thought life
- how these might be used by you to support someone else's well-being.

'Set your minds on things above, not on earthly things.'
(Col. 3:2)

ACT:

Having reflected on God's generosity in the area of our minds, how will you respond?

Consider:

- introducing a new regular practice of prayer and quiet meditation, finding a rhythm and approach that feel natural to you
- preparing a small bag of items which can serve as a 'sacred space' wherever you are. It might include a candle, a holding cross, reflective cards, daily readings, journal and pen. Use the bag as the base cloth on which you set up your chosen objects. As you pray, record any thoughts, phrases or images which come to mind and hold these in your mind throughout the day.
- prioritising 'Sabbath time' every week
- seeking out Bible passages where Jesus exercised effective stewardship of his mind and generosity in his dealings with individuals who were struggling
- organising a regular get-together with people whose company you find uplifting
- speaking to your church leaders about taking steps to promote emotional well-being within your congregation and wider community.

RESOURCES:

Scripture:

Psalms 8 and 139
Ephesians 1:1-2:10
Colossians 3:1-17

Books:

Guy Prentice Waters, **The Sabbath as Rest and Hope for the People of God**, (Wheaton: Crossway, 2022)

Henri Nouwen, **Making All Things New: An Invitation to the Spiritual Life** (New York: HarperOne, 1998)

Sheilah Steven, **Practical Caring: A Handbook for the Pastoral Visitor** (Edinburgh: Scottish Christian Press, 2004)

Websites:

Mind – **mind.org.uk**
See Me – **seemescotland.org**

Case Study

> **"** Night Church is offered as a 'candlelit oasis of calm in a busy and noisy world'.

An Oasis of Calm

Night Church at Stonehouse St Ninian's Local Ecumenical Parish

St Ninian's Church in Stonehouse describes itself as 'a community church with God's love at its heart. We try hard to be a place where everyone is welcomed and all find a place to belong and grow'.

On the first Sunday of each month, from October through to April, the congregation opens its doors in the evening for Night Church. This is a time to think, pray, reflect and contemplate. People can stay for a short time or for the whole session. Night Church is offered as a 'candlelit oasis of calm in a busy and noisy world'. The church building itself is a sacred space which points to the divine. Interactive stations or pieces of art are often used to inspire attendees. The evening concludes with a short time of led worship.

Night Church is non-threatening. It thrives on an atmosphere of welcome and safety. It is for people of all backgrounds, for regulars and one-timers, for seekers and doubters. It is a place where people can connect with their spirituality without fear of embarrassment or of getting it wrong.

The church seeks to have a ministry of presence towards those who may not find it easy to step over the threshold into a busy, noisy, worshipping community where everyone else seems to 'belong'. The minister, the Rev Stewart Cutler, believes that churches need to be deliberate in ensuring they are contributing to people's healthy minds by offering different ways to engage with spirituality.

The congregation also hosts and supports Hope Café, which works hard to tackle the stigma and discrimination faced by people who experience mental health problems. It is intentional about being friendly, welcoming and supportive, and also offers information and training opportunities. Stewart reflects that, during the lockdown in 2020/2021, when the church building was closed and all activities halted due to the pandemic, people in the community would often ask him when the café was opening again. It wasn't the coffee and cake they missed, but the personal interactions, the chat, the laughs, the sharing, the support. Hope Café is a charity in its own right, but the team includes people from the congregation who simply have a heart for others and who exercise that much-needed ministry of presence.

Here's what the regulars say about the Café and Night Church

- 'I come to Night Church to engage and encounter God and myself in the quiet solitude. No chatter or interactions with anyone but Him, and most importantly no demands or expectations. Just me gratefully showing up, quietly reflecting, soaking in all the soothing atmosphere and returning to me.'
- 'Night Church is not a place but an experience. It's spiritual. I love the stillness where I can feel 'the presence of the saints who've gone before' and the nearness of God. The evening meditation is a perfect finish to my day.'
- 'Night Church allows time for personal reflection. It's one of those thin places where we can feel nearer to God.'
- 'For me, Night Church is a quiet still place for contemplation and prayer which provides relief from the noise and busy lives that we lead.'
- 'Hope Café is a safe place which is non-threatening and provides a listening ear. Therapies are available to try in a discreet way. I now volunteer.'
- 'Hope Café is a meeting place for time to chat and, without realising, sorting out some issues you may have.'

For more information on the Night Church and Hope Café visit:
www.st-ninians-stonehouse.org.uk.

VISION

Finding direction and purpose in our lives and in our congregations

> **❝** When we catch glimpses of vision from God, we open ourselves to wholly unexpected possibilities and respond with obedience and gratitude.

Day-by-Day Vision

God has made it possible for us to see the world as God sees it – to recognise where God is calling us, to see ways to serve one another, and to keep our eyes fixed on Christ. Following this vision can help us sense that God is with us on our journey through life.

The Book of Exodus narrates the story of the Israelites' liberation from slavery in Egypt under the leadership of Moses. In chapter 13, the Israelites have just escaped their captors and are fleeing from the Egyptian army. Instead of taking the more direct route out of Egypt, at God's direction they embark on a winding path through the desert and wilderness. This plunges them into unknown territory, leaving behind familiarity and thrusting them into uncertainty.

Throughout our lives, it can sometimes feel like we're lost in the wilderness. Perhaps our sense of purpose has diminished in the face of daily obligations. Perhaps we've enjoyed material success, but still feel a sense of purposelessness at our core. Perhaps a future that we imagined has not come to pass. Where now do we place our hope? The path we were following has disappeared, and we no longer know which way to turn.

We can feel lost in church as well. Perhaps we look around at empty buildings and realise that the way we've always done things is no longer working. We focus only on keeping the lights on or the pulpit filled, and lose sight of our true purpose in Christ. Perhaps we have money and members, but realise that our traditions have excluded others. Perhaps our expression of Church is new and emerging, and we are unsure of what might happen next. We know that we are in uncharted territory, and we find ourselves unable to imagine a path forward.

The Israelites wonder why God is taking them on such a circuitous route to the Promised Land. Indeed, there are plenty of times during their wanderings when they grumble about the path they are on! By directing them in this way, God is helping them avoid war and greater hardship (Ex. 13:17-22). God further protects the Israelites by giving them a guide for the journey: 'By day the Lord went ahead of them in a pillar of cloud to guide them on their way and by night in a pillar of fire to give them light, so that they could travel by day or night. Neither the pillar of cloud by day nor the pillar of fire by night left its place in front of the people.' While they may not have had a full understanding of their route or destination, the Israelites have to trust that by fixing their eyes on God, they will ultimately be led down the right path.

In our own times 'in the wilderness', having faith doesn't mean having a perfect vision of where God is leading us. Instead, like the Israelites, we are called to trust that God will lead us to the next right step, and to the next right step after that. And, like the Israelites, we are not alone on this journey. God has promised to be with us: 'And surely I am with you always, to the very end of the age' (Matt. 28:20). Even when we don't have the full picture, God is there to guide us day by day, making a way out of no way.

Being a steward of 'day-by-day vision' means remaining focussed on God in all our activities. It means having faith in the power of God's word and of prayer, even when our situation seems hopeless. It means trusting that when we find ourselves in a desert of broken dreams – not even knowing how to pray or what to pray for – the Holy Spirit is with us (Rom. 8:26-27). It means watching for a glimmer of inspiration to lead us onto the next step of a new path. It means listening for the wisdom of the Holy Spirit in our conversations, our relationships and our activities. Most of all, when we catch glimpses of vision from God, we open ourselves to wholly unexpected possibilities and respond with obedience and gratitude.

The path God leads us on won't always be easy, and our destination may not be the one we had imagined. God took the Israelites through the wilderness, not down the easy road. We want to believe that God wants us to be happy, safe and successful by worldly standards, but that's not what is promised by this gift of vision. What is promised is that God will be there to lead, support, guide and comfort us. What is promised is that Christ will always serve as our beacon of light. Even though the road may be difficult, with Christ as our leader we can never be lost.

When we steward God's vision, our lives are richer and more fruitful. We take joy in helping to build God's kingdom. Most of all, we do not fear losing our way, because we know that God is beside us always.

THINK/SHARE:

Tell someone or make a note of a time when:

- you asked God to direct your plans or decision making
- you felt God calling you to take a bold step
- your congregation had a vision for mission or outreach and made it happen.

REFLECT:

Reflect on your own experiences or the stories you have heard from others on this theme. Now read Isaiah 25:6-9.

Consider:

- whether God is pointing you or your congregation to a new future
- how grasping God's faithfulness and promise to be with us always impacts your daily life
- what it means to be good stewards of a shared vision for the church.

'In that day they will say, "Surely this is our God; we trusted in him, and he saved us. This is the Lord, we trusted in him; let us rejoice and be glad in his salvation." ' (Isa. 25:9)

ACT:

Having reflected on God's generosity in the area of vision, how will you respond?

Consider:

- writing a hymn, poem or prayer of gratitude to God for the role of hope in your life
- choosing a time to sit in prayer or meditation, asking God to direct your thinking
- meeting with others to pray about a fresh vision for your congregation's future
- encouraging your congregation to explore the emerging needs of the community.

RESOURCES:

Scripture:

Jeremiah 29:10-14
2 Corinthians 1:8-11
2 Corinthians 4:16-18

Books:

Richard Rohr, **The Naked Now: Learning to See as the Mystics See** (New York: Crossroad Publishing, 2009)

Michael Wright, **Yours, Lord: A Handbook of Christian Stewardship** (London: Mowbray, 1992)

Desmond Tutu and Douglas Carlton Abrams, **God's Dream** (Somerville: Candlewick Press, 2008)

David McCarthy, **Seeing Afresh: Learning from Fresh Expressions of Church** (Edinburgh: Saint Andrew Press, 2019)

Case Study

A Vision of Love and Service

Dundonald Parish Church

Dundonald Parish Church has become a shining beacon of love and support in its village in Ayrshire. Driven by its mission to be disciples of Jesus, to praise God and to care for the community, the congregation embarked on serving its neighbours in light of the struggles brought on by the Covid-19 pandemic.

Understanding the importance of approaching their mission with humility and understanding, the minister and congregation engaged in extensive conversations with residents of the village. Their goal was to comprehend the challenges faced by the community and to identify meaningful ways to extend a helping hand.

These conversations inspired the church, leading to numerous initiatives aimed at sharing God's love in diverse and impactful ways. One such initiative involved sending out 'bags of joy' filled with treats and uplifting messages to individuals experiencing isolation within the parish, and to families connected with the local school. They adorned the railings around the church building with the colourful artwork of local children, serving as a visual reminder of hope and resilience.

Expanding their outreach further, the congregation established various specialised ministries. An online school chaplaincy was initiated, ensuring spiritual support for students and staff. A woodland chaplaincy was formed, creating a space for reflection and connection with nature. They also created a men's ministry and a women's walking group, providing platforms for fellowship and personal growth.

However, the most significant undertaking was the establishment of Floyd's, a local food bank and community hub. Through partnerships with other food banks, with the local council and community groups, the congregation extended support to vulnerable people in the area. Floyd's not only provides food but also serves as a safe space for individuals to seek support, advice and care. Visitors to Floyds receive professional support and connections with services such as welfare, housing benefits and mental health support.

The efforts of the church have not gone unnoticed in the wider community which has rallied behind these initiatives. Over half the volunteers at Floyd's come from outwith the church's membership. The local pub generously donates food and space for the men's ministry, while a nearby supermarket contributes to the food bank. Talented individuals from the community have offered their services to redesign the church's website and assist with funding applications, and the church has formed partnerships with key organisations such as GPs and schools, solidifying its position as an invaluable community resource. In turn, more and more people are participating in church activities and curious about faith.

Under the guidance of the Parish Minister, Rev Lynsey Brennan, the congregation strives to fulfil its mission of loving its neighbours unconditionally. This vision has exceeded the church's expectations, leading to remarkable growth and flourishing within the congregation itself, with more than thirty new members joining the church in 2022 and over fifty young people now attending the youth programmes each week.

Lynsey expresses her gratitude, acknowledging that the church's ability to extend extraordinary hospitality stems from the love, grace and compassion of God. By embracing a shared vision and embodying its mission, the congregation has fostered a connected community where love and compassion thrive, and where Christ is glorified.

> "...the church's ability to extend extraordinary hospitality stems from the love, grace and compassion of God.

For more information about Dundonald Parish Church, visit **dundonaldonline.org.uk**.

CONCLUSION

What happens next?

> " God's generosity is transformational, not transactional.

An Attitude of Gratitude

The old saying 'You scratch my back and I'll scratch yours' is a sentiment which is still prevalent today. One friend might say to another, 'Thanks, I owe you one', or at work someone might 'call in a favour' from a colleague. These phrases reveal the transactional nature of giving and receiving in our society: you have given me something, so I must give you something in return.

For thousands of years, societies have been structured according to this principle. Those in positions of power or wealth act as benefactors to the population, who are then understood to owe something (taxes, loyalty, votes…) to the benefactor in return. Gratitude, understood in these terms, is part of a cycle of obligation: a benefactor gives a gift to a beneficiary who must then give something to the benefactor in return, and so on. The downside to such a system is that it often becomes used as a means of patronage, power or control.[15] A gift which must be earned or returned is not much of a gift after all.

With God, however, the story is different. Through each of the chapters of this book, we've considered many of the good gifts God provides across different areas of our lives, and many, many more volumes could be written about all the things that haven't been mentioned here. Yet none of these gifts was given as a means of patronage, power or control. They were given freely out of God's generosity without placing us under any debt, without seeking to coerce or control in any way. It's called 'grace', a word which comes from the same root as the word gratitude.

Diana Butler Bass paints a vivid picture of how she imagines God's generosity:

> When I think of grace, I particularly like the image of God tossing gifts around – a sort of indiscriminate giver of sustenance, joy, love, and pleasure. Grace – gifts given without being earned and with no expectation of return – is, as the old hymn says, amazing.[16]

God's grace does not expect token gifts in return, commodities exchanged to keep the transactional cycle going. Out of grace and generosity, God gives freely. We see this throughout our lives, across creation and ultimately in the incarnation, death and resurrection of Jesus.

This leads us to a different understanding of gratitude. It is not something we have to do to earn or pay back a favour, but is instead a deep thankfulness for what has been given. This sort of gratitude is encouraged by Paul when he writes to an early church in Thessalonica, urging them to 'give thanks in all circumstances; for this is God's will for you in Christ Jesus' (1 Thess. 5:18). Taking time to notice the generosity of God in our lives and to give thanks leads to a deep sense of gratitude and helps us grow in faith. God's generosity is transformational, not transactional.

Gratitude, though, is more than just an inward feeling: it is something which is lived out. Developing a deep appreciation for God's generosity encourages us to live generously too. As people made in God's image and bearing God's name, how do we reflect something of God's grace to the world by giving generously without any expectation of return? Can we give of our money and possessions without asking 'what's in it for me'? Can we give of our time and gifts in service of others without expecting them to 'repay the favour'?

Psalm 24 opens by saying 'The earth is the Lord's, and everything in it'. Living generously means first recognising that all we have is given freely into our care by God, and then seeking to reflect that generosity in how we live our lives. Having considered the blessings of God, generations, relationships, time, volunteers, gifts, money, possessions, earth, body, mind and vision, what happens now? How will you cultivate gratitude for what God provides? And how will that turn into generosity in your life?

THINK/SHARE:

Look back over your journey through the themes of this book. Tell someone or make a note of:

- what you are most grateful for
- something which helped you appreciate God's generosity in a new way
- any perceptions which have changed or new ideas which have been revealed
- what you found most challenging.

REFLECT:

Reflect on what has been thought about or shared. Now read Colossians 2:1-7.

Consider:

- how generosity might help you live your life in Christ
- what helps root you in Christ and in your Christian community
- in what ways recognising God's generosity and living generously can help strengthen your faith
- what makes you 'overflow with thankfulness'.

'So then, just as you received Christ Jesus as Lord, continue to live your lives in him, rooted and built up in him, strengthened in the faith as you were taught, and overflowing with thankfulness.' (Col. 2:6-7)

ACT:

Having reflected on God's generosity, how will you respond?

Consider:

- committing to an act of generosity in one or more areas of your life
- being more intentional about noticing what you are grateful for
- developing a regular practice of giving generously.

Use this space to make a note of three things which will change in your life as a result of working through this book:

1.

2.

3.

You could commit these things to God using a simple prayer:

Generous God,
Thank you for all the good things you freely give, especially for ___.
Help me to live in a way which reflects your generosity.
With your help, I commit to ___.
Amen

RESOURCES:

Books:

Adam J. Copeland (ed.), **Beyond the Offering Plate: A Holistic Approach to Stewardship** (Louisville: Westminster John Knox Press, 2017)

Mark Allan Powell, **Giving to God: The Bible's Good News about Living a Generous Life** (Grand Rapids: Eerdmans, 2006)

Robert Schnase, **Practicing Extravagant Generosity: Daily Readings on the Grace of Giving** (Nashville: Abingdon Press, 2011)

Michael Wright, **Yours, Lord: A Handbook of Christian Stewardship** (London: Mowbray, 1992)

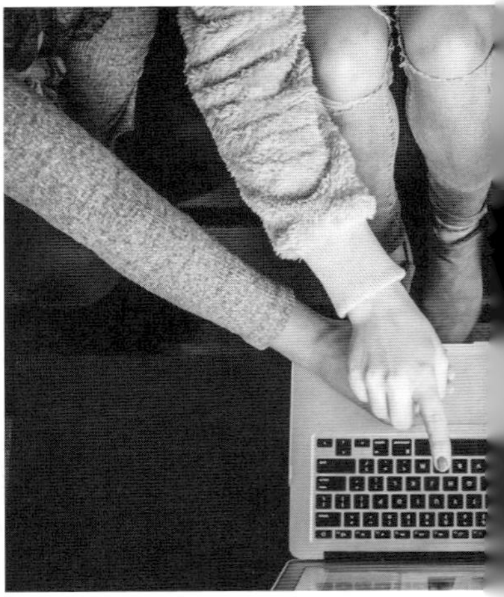

The Church of Scotland
Stewardship & Finance Department
A NARRATIVE OF GENEROSITY
INTRODUCTION
the Narrative of Generosity resources to
whole-life approach to stewardship

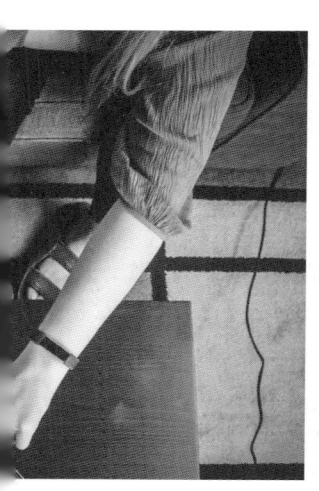

A Narrative of Generosity

To help you explore the themes of this book further, the Church of Scotland's National Stewardship Team has prepared a set of free digital resources called **A Narrative of Generosity**.

For each theme, they can provide:

- an introduction
- share, reflect, act questions and slides
- worship materials
- four-part Bible study
- four-part devotional
- resources for use with children, young people and intergenerationally.

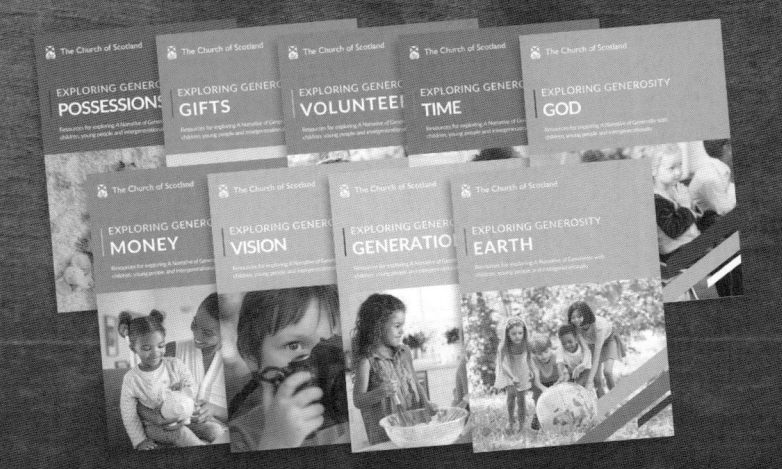

Contact **stewardship@churchofscotland.org.uk** for more information.

Endnotes

1. Breanna Alverson, 'Weekly Devotional: My Diamond. My Rock. My Forever', Grand Canyon University, September 15, 2017, https://www.gcu.edu/blog/spiritual-life/weekly-devotional-my-diamond-my-rock-my-forever.

2. Kara E. Powell, Brad M. Griffin and Cheryl A. Crawford, *Sticky Faith Youth Worker Edition: Practical Ideas to Nurture Long-term Faith in Teenagers*, (Grand Rapids: Zondervan, 2011), p. 79.

3. C. S. Lewis, *Mere Christianity* (New York: MacMillan, 1960), p. 120.

4. Michael Battle (ed.), *The Wisdom of Desmond Tutu* (Oxford: Lion Publishing, 1998), p. 38.

5. Andrew Stanley, 'Global Inequalities Report', International Monetary Fund, March 2022, https://www.imf.org/en/Publications/fandd/issues/2022/03/Global-inequalities-Stanley.

6. Dave Davies, 'Trees Talk To Each Other. "Mother Tree" Ecologist Hears Lessons For People Too', Health News from NPR, May 4, 2021, https://www.npr.org/sections/health-shots/2021/05/04/993430007/trees-talk-to-each-other-mother-tree-ecologist-hears-lessons-for-people-too.

7. 'The Anglican Communion's Five Marks of Mission: An Introduction', Anglican Communion News Service, February 4, 2020, https://www.anglicannews.org/features/2020/02/the-anglican-communions-five-marks-of-mission-an-introduction.aspx.

8. Rachel Rettner and Scott Dutfield, 'The Human Body: Anatomy, Facts & Functions', Live Science, December 17, 2021, https://www.livescience.com/37009-human-body.html.

9. Tia Ghose, 'The Human Brain's Memory Could Store the Entire Internet', Live Science, February 18, 2016, https://www.livescience.com/53751-brain-could-store-internet.html.

10. Amy Kenny, *My Body is Not a Prayer Request: Disability Justice in the Church* (Grand Rapids: Brazos Press, 2022), pp. 84–5.

11. See, for example, 'The Health Benefits of Strong Relationships', Harvard Health Publishing, accessed September 22, 2023, https://www.health.harvard.edu/staying-healthy/the-health-benefits-of-strong-relationships.

12. Rachel Held Evans, *Searching for Sunday: Loving, Leaving, and Finding the Church* (Nashville: Nelson, 2015), p. 208.

13. Caroline Leaf, 'How Are The Mind & The Brain Different? A Neuroscientist Explains', MBG Health, March 8, 2021, https://www.mindbodygreen.com/articles/difference-between-mind-and-brain-neuroscientist.

14. See, for example, Paul S. Mueller, David J. Plevak and Teresa A. Rummans, 'Religious Involvement, Spirituality and Medicine: Implications for Clinical Practice', *Mayo Clinic Proceedings* 76 (December 2001): 1125–235, https://www.mayoclinicproceedings.org/article/S0025-6196(11)62799-7/pdf.

15. Diana Butler Bass, *Gratitude: The Transformative Power of Giving Thanks* (San Francisco: HarperOne, 2018), p. 10.

16. Butler Bass, *Gratitude*, p. 19.

Scripture Index

Genesis
1-2   9, 65
1:27-31   71
3:8   25
9:8-17   65

Exodus
1-40   25
13   83

Deuteronomy
4:1-31   13
4:9   19
6:6-7   19

1 Samuel
16:1-7   72

1 Chronicles
29:1-20   53

Job
38-39   65

Psalms
1   13
8   79
8:5   77
24:1a   89
65:8   63
103   12
104   64
104:24-25   63
139   79
139:1-6   77
139:14   71, 77
145   21

Proverbs
11:28   59
16:3   33
16:9   33

Ecclesiastes
3:1   33
3:11   33
5:19   57

Isaiah
25:6-9   84
58   53
65:24   61

Jeremiah
29:10-14   85

Daniel
1   71

Joel
2:28   19

Matthew
4:18-22   25
5:3-10   77
5:13-16   39
6:19-21   58
6:25-30   9
9:21   57
16:24-26   59
22:37   77
25:14-30   53
25:31-46   25
25:35-40   41
25:40   61
28:20   83

Mark
2:23-28   35
10:45   39
10:46-52   25

Luke
2:41-50   19
8:1-3   39
12:1-48   57, 59
18:9-14   51
19:1-9   25
21:1-4   53
22:26-27   39
24:13-35   25

John
3:16   9
13:34-35   27

Acts
9:36-39   39
9:36-42   45

Romans
8:26-27   83
12:1-2   73
12:3-13   47

1 Corinthians
2:11   77
3:16   71
6:12-20   73
6:19   71
10:31-33   73
12:12-27   20
13:1-7   27
13:12   11
16:1-2   53

2 Corinthians
1:4   25
1:8-11   85
4:16-18   85
9:6-15   52

Galatians
5:22-23   23, 25, 78
6:7-10   35
6:10   39

Ephesians
1:1-2:10   79
1:3-4   77
2:10   39
3:17-19   11
3:18b-19   7
4:7-13   46
4:11-13   37
4:25-32   27
5:8-20   34

Philippians
2:1-11   26
4:4-9   13
4:6-7   77

Colossians
2:1-7   90
3:1-2   77
3:1-17   79
3:23-24   41

1 Thessalonians
5:18   89

1 Timothy
6:17-18   9
6:17-19   53

Hebrews
10:19-25   13

James
2:15-17   39

1 Peter
4:7-11   47

1 John
3:16-18   40
3:22-24   40

First published in 2024 by
Saint Andrew Press
121 George Street
Edinburgh EH2 4YN

Copyright © The Church of Scotland 2024

ISBN 978-1-80083-049-3

All rights reserved. No part of this publication may be reproduced or transmitted in any form or by any means, electronic or mechanical, including photocopy, recording, or information storage and retrieval system, without permission in writing from the publisher. This book is sold subject to the condition that it shall not, by way of trade or otherwise, be lent, resold, hired out or otherwise circulated without the publisher's prior consent.

The right of Fiona Penny, Darren Philip, Katherine Southern and Pauline Wilson to be identified as the authors of this work has been asserted in accordance with the Copyright, Designs and Patents Act 1988.

Scripture quotations are from the Holy Bible, New International Version.
Copyright © 1973, 1978, 1984, 2011 by Biblica, Inc.
Used by permission of Zondervan. All rights reserved worldwide.

British Library Cataloguing in Publication Data

A catalogue record for this book is available from the British Library.

It is the publisher's policy to only use papers that are natural and recyclable and that have been manufactured from timber grown in renewable, properly managed forests. All of the manufacturing processes of the papers are expected to conform to the environmental regulations of the country of origin.

Typeset by Chris Flexen, The Church of Scotland

Printed and bound in the United Kingdom by CPI Group (UK) Ltd